Mercy
in the
Teachings
of the **Popes**

PONTIFICAL COUNCIL FOR THE PROMOTION
OF THE NEW EVANGELIZATION

Jubilee of Mercy
2015-2016

Our Sunday Visitor Publishing Division
Our Sunday Visitor, Inc.
Huntington, Indiana 46750

Copyright © 2015 Pontifical Council for the
Promotion of the New Evangelization
Vatican City

Published 2015 by Our Sunday Visitor
Publishing Division

20 19 18 17 16 15   1 2 3 4 5 6 7 8 9

Our Sunday Visitor Publishing Division, Our Sunday Visitor, Inc., 200 Noll Plaza, Huntington, IN 46750; 1-800-348-2440

ISBN: 978-1-61278-980-4 (Inventory No. T1740)
eISBN: 978-1-61278-988-0
LCCN: 2015951030

Translation: Gary Seromik
Cover design: Lindsey Riesen
Cover art: Shutterstock; Pontifical Council for the
Promotion of the New Evangelization
Interior design: Sherri L. Hoffman

PRINTED IN THE UNITED STATES OF AMERICA

TABLE OF CONTENTS

PREFACE

In *Misericordiae Vultus*, the bull of indiction of the extraordinary Jubilee of Mercy, Pope Francis cites three popes, highlighting the special interest each had concerning the theme of mercy. He refers, first of all, to Pope John XXIII who, upon opening the Second Vatican Council, said: "Now the Bride of Christ wishes to use the medicine of mercy rather than taking up arms of severity.... The Catholic Church, as she holds high the torch of Catholic truth at this Ecumenical Council, wants to show herself a loving mother to all: patient, kind, moved by compassion and goodness toward her separated children." The second is Pope Paul VI who, at the conclusion of Vatican II, noted the extent to which the parable of the Good Samaritan served as a model for the council's teaching. Finally, he summarizes Pope John Paul II's teachings in this regard as presented in his encyclical *Dives in Misericordia*.

These examples have served as a catalyst for gathering together in a short summary the richness of the teachings of recent popes on the central message of the upcoming Jubilee. An incredible wealth emerges from these teachings because mercy penetrates all areas of the life of the Church as well as the life of every Christian. The beautiful passages that follow are a precious testimony of the extent to which references to mercy have been constant throughout the ages in the teachings of the Church. The Pontifical Council for the

Promotion of the New Evangelization is grateful to Dr. Laurent Touze, a professor at the Pontifical University of the Holy Cross, for having contributed this selection to point out that mercy has been central to the teachings of recent popes. Our only regret is that we are not able to publish all the material on this subject, which is both extraordinary and rich, yet whose dimensions far surpass those needed for having a concise and ready-to-use pastoral tool to prepare for the Jubilee. We are confident that pondering these pages will lead not only to a reflection on the importance of mercy, but will serve as an impetus so that mercy becomes part of the daily life of every believer in carrying out his responsibility to be a credible witness to the Gospel.

✠ Rino Fisichella
President, Pontifical Council for the
Promotion of the New Evangelization

INTRODUCTION

Preaching Mercy, a Basis for Contemporary Papal Teachings

The popes and mercy. This anthology is situated at the point where these two lines intersect — two lines among many others — which have left their mark on the life of the Catholic Church during the last hundred years. On one hand, for the past hundred years at least, popes have played a much more important role than their predecessors in giving practical guidance to the spiritual life of the faithful. Thanks in part to the teachings of the successors of St. Peter, the way in which people pray and proclaim the Gospel is more intense today than ever. On the other hand, there is a greater awareness of the presence of God's mercy throughout our life in Jesus Christ. There is no doubt that God himself has instilled this awareness in the hearts of his children — for example, the way in which they freely follow the inspiration of the Holy Spirit and the poignant way in which they discover the messages focused on divine mercy like those of St. Thérèse of Lisieux and St. Faustina Kowalska. Nonetheless, this awareness has also been propagated by the numerous teachings of the popes that present the Paschal Mystery as a mystery of mercy, using language appropriate to their particular period of time.

Thus, for nearly a century — or rather two — the popes have exercised a strong influence on the spirituality of Catholics throughout the world. In a certain sense, this has always been the case, since, for example, Christians throughout the ages have attended Mass, which is at the root and the center of Christian life (see *Presbyterorum Ordinis*, 14), in union with the Bishop of Rome, who is cited in the Canon of the Mass, and have regularly received from the Apostolic See new liturgical measures that have shaped their spiritual life, as well as new saints to imitate, etc. However, during the nineteenth and twentieth centuries, in addition to these traditional dimensions of the faith, the popes began to promote the Christian life in a more genuine way, in a way that was much more concrete and incisive than in previous eras. Here are a few of the many examples: Pope Leo XIII wrote sixteen important documents on the Rosary, eleven of which were encyclicals, in order to help spread this particular Marian devotion; Pope St. Pius X, by encouraging the frequent reception of holy Communion, became one of the greatest reformers of the internal life of the Church since the Council of Trent; and Pope Pius XI, in his encyclical *Mens Nostra*, published in 1929, encouraged the dissemination of St. Ignatius' Spiritual Exercises. Moreover, there were the various holy years, as well as the Marian years, such as those that Pope Pius XII proclaimed in 1954 and Pope St. John Paul II proclaimed in 1987, as well as the three years of preparation that he proclaimed for the Jubilee of the year 2000, which were dedicated to the Persons of the Holy Trinity.

There are many reasons why popes now have more direct contact with Catholics throughout the world. For example, there is the evolution in technology. Traveling is much easier, both for the pope traveling from Rome and for the faithful traveling to Rome. Radio, television, as well as many other new technological advances in communications today, allow Christians to follow what the pope is saying in real time. There are other reasons that are more political and social in nature. With the disappearance of the so-called Catholic powers, the door was opened for the Holy See to have more direct contact with the people. At the end of the old regime, in the period just prior to the French Revolution, governments — such as the Habsburg state in Northern Italy — felt responsible in part for the pastoral care of their people. After the Revolution, though, political authorities were often openly anti-Christian, thereby leading to a deeper and more active spiritual bond between the papacy and the Catholic laity. In order to address the faithful, the pope no longer relied on a civil mediator. Moreover, within this context of direct dialogue, the popes of recent times have often placed greater emphasis on the holiness of the laity. In addition, faced with challenges they share in common on a global scale, Christians have become increasingly aware of the need for a certain unity in their pastoral and apostolic response to these challenges, and thus for unity with Rome. Finally, the persecutions the popes have suffered since that time, beginning with Pope Pius VI and extending to those who were "prisoners of the Vatican" after 1870, along with the attempt on Pope John Paul II's life, the long illness he suffered afterward and the reaction generated by Pope Benedict XVI's resignation, have led to a deeper affection for the papacy and greater freedom to talk about loyalty to the pope.

This is, therefore, the first point of this anthology: In recent times, the Bishops of Rome have exercised a more active and encompassing spiritual direction over the lives of the faithful throughout the world than their predecessors. The second point is this: The Church, for some time now, has been listening in a renewed way to the message of mercy. Indeed, speaking to the priests of the diocese of Rome on March 6, 2014, Pope Francis said: "Thus we understand that we are ... here ... to hear the voice of the Spirit speaking to the whole Church of our time, which is the time of mercy. I am sure of this ... we are living in a time of mercy, and have been for thirty years or more, up to today.... This was an intuition of John Paul II. He 'sensed' that this was the time of mercy."

Thus this time of mercy began at least thirty years ago, back in the early years of the pontificate of St. John Paul II, who was, in a special way, an apostle of divine mercy, thanks to the message of St. Faustina. However, Pope Francis qualified his remark by adding,

"Thirty years *or more*," thereby allowing yet another date for the beginning of this time of mercy.

Indeed, for over a century we can observe in the message of the popes who have ascended to the Chair of Peter a certain number of characteristics that have led them to often speak about mercy. First and foremost, there is an explicit Christocentrism. The Church's teachings and pastoral approach have always been Christocentric, but have become more instinctively so in more recent times. This Christocentrism points to Christ as the presence of the Father's love throughout history and as the object of man's love. In this sense, there is a somewhat common thread of Christ-centered mercy that unites, for example, the proclamation of the Heart of Jesus, fundamental to the papal magisterium of the late 19th century up to the 1950s; the proclamation of the kingdom of Christ, which Pope Pius XI particularly cherished; the proposals regarding the Christian mystery that the two popes who presided over the Second Vatican Council sought to put forth in patience and in dialogue; the "civilization of love" that Blessed Paul VI preached; charity, which Pope Benedict XVI highlighted; and mercy, which Popes John Paul II and Francis have proclaimed in a very direct way.

Likewise, we can apply Blessed John Henry Newman's enlightening observation regarding the history of spirituality to this continuity of papal teaching: "What the Catholic Church once has had, she never has lost…. Instead of passing from one stage of life to another, she has carried her youth and middle age along with her, on to her latest time…. She did not lose Benedict by finding Dominic; and she has still both Benedict and Dominic at home, though she has become the mother of Ignatius" (*The Mission of the Benedictine Order*). The Church does not lose the preaching on the Heart of Jesus when she pays greater attention to spreading the Kingdom, and she does not forsake her dreams for a civilization of love when she seeks to convert to mercy. At the same time, this continuity — fidelity to the Word of which the pope and the college of bishops are the servants — does not hide the plurality of accents heard and measures taken. Throughout history, the Vicar of Christ and shepherd of the universal Church has sought to read the signs of the times, to listen to what the Spirit is saying to the churches, and to point out the true path to God's people.

This preaching of mercy with its multiple accents has, therefore, as an effect — or perhaps rather as a cause — a message that is essentially Christocentric. By no means was papal teaching prior to our modern era solely disciplinary in nature. However, over the last two centuries it has acquired a tone that is more pastoral and missionary in nature, speaking first and foremost about Christ in a more direct way. This teaching seeks, first of all, to present Christ to mankind, and to present him in a way that is more biblically based and more apostolically convincing. It highlights God's merciful love, manifested throughout history in Jesus Christ.

The pastoral decisions the popes have made are part of a broader Christocentric movement in the Church and are choices they themselves have only partially made: it is the Holy Spirit who gives the faithful an instinct to discover — for example through popular devotions — new roads that will always lead them to Christ (see *Evangelii Gaudium*, 31, 119, 122-126). We will briefly illustrate some concrete manifestations of this Christocentrism as it has been lived out, focusing especially on two points: first, the spirituality of the nineteenth century as the first fruits of what will be the spirituality of the twentieth century and the very beginning of the twenty-first century, which we will observe in the quotations from the papal teachings in this anthology; and, second, the way in which popular devotion is intertwined with encouragement from the hierarchy.

Indeed, one might say that the nineteenth century was a "rediscovery" of Christ, thereby shaping the mindset of Catholics during the following two centuries, and that it was a rediscovery of a perfectly loving Christ. Two examples come to mind: deeper friendship with Christ through the Eucharist and trust in the Sacred Heart.

Friendship with Christ present in the Eucharist spread among Christians with the advent of frequent Communion. This movement gradually took shape in a marked way during the pontificate of Blessed Pius IX (1846-78). Various factors contributed to this progressive change. First, there were the books that the faithful avidly read, books that were simple and short, such as those of Bishop Gaston Adrien de Ségur (d. 1881), who was the son of Countess Sophie Rostopchine, the author of several famous children's novels. A former judge of the Roman Rota who returned to France upon losing his eyesight, Bishop de Ségur became one of the most sought-out confessors in Paris. In 1858, he met the Curé of Ars (St. John Vianney), who said, "This is a blind man who sees more clearly than we do" and "Today, I saw a saint." Bishop de Ségur published numerous religious works that were often translated, including a treatise on *The Most Holy Communion* in 1860 which sold hundreds of thousands of copies and whose essential message was "We do not partake of Communion because we are good, but to become better." Pope Pius IX himself praised the book and gave a copy as a gift to each preacher in Rome during Lent 1862.

Books advocating frequent Communion have their origin first of all in Italy. Most notable are the books of Venerable Giuseppe Frassinetti, founder of the Congregation of the Sons of Holy Mary Immaculate who died in 1868, especially his book *Il convito del divino amore [The Banquet of Divine Love]* (Genoa, 1867), and of St. John Bosco, especially his book *Il giovane provveduto per la pratica de' suoi doveri degli esercizi di cristiana pieta [The Young Man Led by the Practice of His Duty to Exercise Christian Devotion]* (Turin, 1847), which was reprinted numerous times. This book, along with the pastoral approach of Don Bosco, the founder of the Salesians, represents a movement that is much broader and revealing: the Spirit and the Church together encouraging frequent Communion *and* frequent confession, fully aware of the bonds that unite these two sacraments (see *Catechism of the Catholic Church*, 1457-58).

In addition to these books, the popes took certain measures that encouraged frequent Communion, such as Pope Leo XIII's encyclical *Mirae Caritatis* (May 28, 1902) and especially St. Pius

X's decree *Sacra Tridentina Synodus* (December 20, 1905), which encouraged even daily Communion. In this same vein, the Holy See urged bishops not to withhold first Communion from very young children. Under Pope Pius IX, the Vatican corrected certain provisions that a few local councils and some French prelates had made in this regard. However, the greatest change for reception of Communion by young children was the result of Pope Pius X's decree *Quam Singulari* (August 8, 1910): the age of reason was set at seven years and it was sufficient for a child to be familiar with the principal mysteries of the faith and to make a distinction between the bread of the Eucharist and ordinary bread. These provisions were also included in what is known as the "Catechism of St. Pius X," which enjoyed tremendous popularity.

More frequent reception of the Eucharist over the last two centuries illustrates this growing Christocentric awareness among the faithful. Devotion to the Sacred Heart — especially during the period of 1800 to 1950 — is yet another example of this renewed awareness of the love of the triune God for man. According to the often cited words of Msgr. Maurice d'Hulst, the founder and first rector of the Catholic Institute of Paris, who died in 1896, the nineteenth century was indeed, "when considered from a mystical point of view ... the century of the Sacred Heart."

There certainly exists a body of negative literature on this devotion, oftentimes based on certain manifestations that were sentimental and even upsetting, presenting God the Father as thirsty for the blood of Christ and Christians. However, it would be more fitting to try to understand how much this devotion has helped destroy any illusion of salvation without human cooperation, thereby spreading among Christians a yearning to freely adhere to God's love and to spread salvation throughout the world, especially through apostolic missions and an active concern for the poor. Loving contemplation of the Heart of Jesus enabled this teaching on salvation to reach the hearts and minds of the faithful.

This devotion was first and foremost the fruit of a certain

spiritual self-determination on the part of the faithful, rather than the result of any encouragement from the hierarchy. On the contrary, at the end of the seventeenth century, reeling from the crisis caused by Quietism, the Holy See refused to recognize any new type of devotion. It is only in the eighteenth century that the Holy See lent its support to devotion to the Sacred Heart as an antidote to the vague ideas of theism and some lingering Jansenistic trends. Pope Clement XIII instituted the liturgical feast in 1765 at the request of Polish bishops, and Pope Pius IX extended its observance to the entire Church in 1856. Margaret Mary Alacoque, the visionary of the Sacred Heart at Paray-le-Monial who died in 1690, was beatified in 1864 and canonized in 1920.

In this movement, which promoted acts of consecration to the Sacred Heart, the papacy followed the rest of the faithful rather than preceding them. The first examples of nations making such an act of consecration occurred in Belgium on the eve of Vatican I, when Cardinal Victor Auguste Dechamps entrusted the nation to the Heart of Christ, and in Ecuador, when the president of that country, Gabriel García Moreno, consecrated it in 1873. It is only later that Pope Leo XIII, encouraged by Sister Maria Droste zu Vischering, known as Blessed Mary of the Divine Heart, made the consecration for the entire world, an event marked by his encyclical on consecration to the Sacred Heart, *Annum Sacrum* (May 25, 1899). Later, in 1902, Colombia was also consecrated to the Sacred Heart, a gesture repeated by each of its heads of state until 1994. Finally, King Alfonso XIII entrusted Spain to the Sacred Heart in 1919.

Devotion to the Heart of Christ perfectly illustrates the transition from the cold, stark theism of the eighteenth century to an awareness of the loving presence of the Trinity in the hearts of the faithful, the transition from a religion of duty to a religion of love. Its language of heartfelt sentiment must not be confused with that of sentimentalism: it opened the doors to the development of a Christianity of the heart in a truly evangelical spirit that is still alive today among Christians. This transition from an attitude of indifference to one of concern, and the beginning, therefore, of this time of mercy, is associated with the pontificate of Blessed Pius IX. During his pontificate, preaching God's mercy was envisioned as a way of overcoming Jansenistic tendencies that were still prevalent in the spirituality of certain Catholics. The issue was no longer that of the doctrinal Jansenism of the seventeenth century, but rather a spiritual Jansenism characterized by a severity and seriousness in a religion imbued with a sense of duty that was somewhat akin to philosophical Kantianism or Protestant Victorianism. This can be seen, for example, at the dawn of the modern era in the case of Italian Bishop Scipione de' Ricci and statements from the synod he held at Pistoia (1786-1787), which were subsequently condemned by Pope Pius VI in his papal bull entitled *Auctorem Fidei* of August 28, 1794. Bishop Ricci had printed certain works by some of the leading Jansenistic authors of Port Royal (Antoine Arnauld and Pierre Nicole), works opposed to devotion to the Sacred Heart that introduced unwarranted distinctions in the person of the Incarnate Word, as well as still other books that maintained the total corruption of human nature because of original sin and called for rigorous penitential practices. By taking a more prominent role in the formation of everyday spirituality, the popes were able to gradually contain these Jansenistic tendencies.

The spread of St. Alphonsus Liguori's moral teachings is one of the manifestations and one of the causes of this rejection of rigorism in the nineteenth century, especially among the clergy. Founder of the Redemptorists, he died in 1787, was beatified in 1816, was canonized in 1839, and was declared a Doctor of the Church in 1871. His profound moral reflections, which were propagated with the encouragement of the Apostolic See, paved the way for overcoming some rigorous pastoral practices prevalent among the clergy. When Alphonsus entered religious life in 1723, rigorism played an important role in Catholic pastoral practice, a consequence of the battle against Quietism — the hierarchy sought to promote the practical daily obligations of a moral way of life as opposed to the excesses of pseudo-mysticism — as well as the battle against Jansenism — there was no desire to give way to the laxism of which the Jansenists accused the Church, especially the Jesuits. Thus St. Alphonsus sought to make it easier for the faithful to encounter God's love through a piety that was simple and loving.

This way in which St. Alphonsus' solutions progressively made inroads among the clergy is best illustrated by the example of the Curé of Ars. St. John Vianney learned about St. Alphonsus through his bishop, the Most Rev. Alexandre Devie, who published a pastoral letter in 1830 praising St. Alphonsus' *Theologia Moralis*. Every winter, this holy priest studied his personal copy of *Moral Theology for Use by Priests and Confessors* (1844), which was written by Cardinal Thomas Gousset, the Archbishop of Reims, to present St. Alphonsus' teachings in popular form.

By 1839, St. John Vianney had completely abandoned his former rigorist practices. If he found that penitents were truly contrite, he no longer hesitated to grant them absolution, and he preached in a more encouraging way, almost always on divine love. For example, he said: "How good God is! His good heart is an ocean of mercy. Even though we may be great sinners, let us never despair of our salvation. It is so easy to be saved!"; "Our sins are like grains of sand next to God's mercies"; "What are our sins, if we compare them to God's mercies! They are like little seeds next to a mountain"; "God runs after the man and makes him come back"; and, "The Jansenists still have the sacraments, but they serve no purpose because they believe a person has to be too perfect to receive them. The Church desires our salvation; that's why she requires us to receive the sacraments."

The saint combined this abandonment of rigorism with a deep sense of the reparation that was due for the sins he had absolved, with a strong horror of sin: "Oh my Jesus, give us a holy horror for our sins. Instill into our hearts a drop of bitterness with which your heart was inundated. If we cannot wipe out our sins through the shedding of our blood, at least make us weep for them." We must never see his abandonment of rigorism as conversion to laxism or permissiveness!

Finally, when considering the ways in which devotion to a suffering and merciful Christ was spread among Christians, most notably those that Christians find instinctively attractive because they recognize therein the essence of the Gospel, our thoughts turn, first of all, to those works of devotion that were widely read by the faithful. *The Imitation of Christ* serves as one example of such literature throughout the first part of the last century until the 1950s. During this period, *The Imitation of Christ* reached an audience that had never been reached before and soon became the book that was read by every Christian who had a taste for spiritual things.

The apologist Joseph de Maistre from Turin, Italy, who died in 1821, read it, as did the Venerable Pauline Jaricot, founder of the Society of the Propagation of the Faith, who died in 1862. Blessed Frédéric Ozanam (d. 1853), whose Society of St. Vincent de Paul, which he established in 1833, would begin every meeting with a reading from this book. This book not only reached the more privileged sectors of society; it was equally popular among the working classes. The famous Provençal poet Frédéric Mistral, recipient of the Nobel Prize in Literature who died in 1914, for example, tells about his father, a peasant who fought in Napoleon's wars, who had read only three books in his lifetime: the *New Testament*, *The Imitation of Christ*, and *Don Quixote* (which reminded him of Napoleon's campaign in Spain and served as a distraction when the rains came).

Another means by which the proclamation of a merciful Christ was able to reach the masses was through the preaching that took place at missions to the people, which actually began well before our modern period, and which *Misericordiae Vultus* explicitly mentions as an apostolic outreach that needs to be rediscovered. The Franciscan friar St. Leonard of Port Maurice (d. 1751) offers an example of this. He preached more than three hundred of these missions in eighteenth-century Italy, and everywhere he went the attendance of the faithful was overwhelming. In his sermons, he preferred to speak about the Mother of Mercy instead of hell, because he was convinced it was easier to convert sinners in this way. He also built nearly six hundred Stations of the Cross and promoted devotion to the Sacred Heart.

———

This is the historical context for the texts of the popes contained in this anthology. The choice of quotations should be seen as an invitation to further reading: I was often tempted to transcribe everything in its entirety, but these extracts should stir up a desire to delve deeper into the original texts.

Since another work in this same collection deals with mercy in the Bible, the analysis of scriptural texts on this theme are not included here, even though the popes often discuss them in their works — for example, Pope John Paul II in the fourth book of this collection (on the Old Testament) and in the fifth book (on the parable of the prodigal son), based on his encyclical *Dives in Misericordia*. Moreover, since this book focuses directly on the bishops of Rome, it does not directly deal with the texts of the Second Vatican Council on mercy or with other important documents such as the *Catechism of the Catholic Church*. As regards the span of time under consideration, it starts with the pontificate of Pope Pius XI (elected February 6, 1922) and ends with Pope Francis' bull of indiction on the extraordinary Jubilee of Mercy (*Misericordiae Vultus*, April 11, 2015).

CHAPTER ONE

Mercy in the Teachings of the Popes

Preaching focused on mercy is one aspect of papal teaching, which aims to proclaim the love of God and the essence of the Gospel in a way that is specifically adapted to our times, as Pope John Paul II often emphasized, just as popes did years before by encouraging Christians to contemplate the Heart of Christ and to work together toward establishing God's kingdom.

The Popes' Goal: Preaching the Heart of the Gospel

The goal of the papal magisterium is to be an echo of the Incarnate Word, preaching that is centered on love (see Mt 22:34-40, for example). This emphasis on love was, in a special way, the driving force behind the pastoral agenda of Vatican II, as Pope John XXIII and his successors presented it.

Pius XI: Devotion to the Sacred Heart

Devotion to the Sacred Heart contains the substance of our faith, insofar as it facilitates our love for Christ and our imitation of him: "For is not the sum of all religion and therefore the pattern of more perfect life, contained in that most auspicious sign [devotion to the Sacred Heart] and in the form of piety that follows from it inasmuch as it more readily leads the minds of men to an intimate knowledge of Christ our Lord, and more efficaciously moves their hearts to love him more vehemently and to imitate him more closely?" (*Miserentissimus Redemptor*, 3, May 8, 1928).

John XXIII: Mercy and the plan for the council

Even before his election as pope, St. John XXIII — Giuseppe Roncalli — was convinced that the proclamation of mercy should be at the heart of the life of the Church. Therefore, he refers to God's mercy in several places throughout the intimate journal he kept during the spiritual exercises he made in 1940 in Terapia on the Bosphorus. In his journal, he quotes *Esposizione del 'Miserere*, which was published by Father Paolo Segneri, S.J., who died in 1694, and which is also the source for certain quotes and expression of the future pope.

"Tuesday, November 26[:]… *The great mercy*. It is not just ordinary mercy that is needed here. The burden of social and personal wickedness is so grave that an ordinary gesture of love does not suffice for forgiveness. So we invoke the great mercy. This is proportionate to the greatness of God. 'For according to his greatness, so also is his mercy' (Eccl 2:23). It is well said that our sins are the seat of divine mercy. It is better said that God's most beautiful name and title is this: mercy. This must inspire us with a great hope amidst our tears. 'Yet mercy triumphs over judgment' (*Exercises*, nos. 48 and 55). This seems too much to hope for. But it cannot be too much if the whole mystery of the Redemption hinges on this: the exercise of mercy is to be a portent of predestination and salvation" (*Journal of a Soul*, 240, McGraw-Hill Book Company: New York, 1964, 1965).

"At the outset of the Second Vatican Council, it is evident, as always, that the truth of the Lord will remain forever. We see, in fact, as one age succeeds another, that the opinions of men follow one another and exclude each other. And often errors vanish as quickly as they arise, like fog before the sun. The Church has always opposed these errors. Frequently she has condemned them with the greatest severity. Nowadays, however, the Spouse of Christ prefers to make use of the medicine of mercy rather than that of severity. She considers that she meets the needs of the present day by demonstrating the validity of her teachings rather than by condemnations.... That being so, the Catholic Church, raising the torch of religious truth by means of this Ecumenical Council, desires to show herself to be the loving mother of all, benign, patient, full of mercy and goodness toward the brethren who are separated from her" (*Opening Speech for the Second Vatican Council*, October 11, 1962).

Paul VI: Charity, the spirituality of Vatican II

"We prefer to point out how charity has been the principal religious feature of this Council. Now, no one can reprove as want of religion or infidelity to the Gospel such a basic orientation, when we recall that it is Christ himself who taught us that love for our brothers is the distinctive mark of his disciples.... The old story of the Samaritan has been the model of the spirituality of the Council. A feeling of boundless sympathy has permeated the whole of it.... A wave of affection and admiration flowed from the Council over the modern world of humanity. Errors were condemned, indeed, because charity demanded this no less than did truth, but for the persons themselves there was only warning, respect, and love" (*Address of Pope Paul VI During the Last General Meeting of the Second Vatican Council*, December 7, 1965).

John Paul II: The mission of the Church is to live and proclaim mercy

"The contemporary Church is profoundly conscious that only on the basis of the mercy of God will she be able to carry out the tasks that derive from the teachings of the Second Vatican Council, and, in the first place, the ecumenical task which aims at uniting all those who confess Christ. As she makes many efforts in this direction, the Church confesses with humility that only that love which is more powerful than the weakness of human divisions can definitively bring about that unity which Christ implored from the Father and which the Spirit never ceases to beseech for us 'with sighs too deep for words'" (*Dives in Misericordia*, 13, November 30, 1980).

"In continuing the great task of implementing the Second Vatican Council, in which we can rightly see a new phase of the self-realization of the Church — in keeping with the epoch in which it has been our destiny to live — the Church herself must be constantly guided by the full consciousness that in this work it is not permissible for her, for any reason, to withdraw into herself. The reason for her existence is, in fact, to reveal God, that Father who allows us to 'see' him in Christ. No matter how strong the resistance of human history may be, no matter how marked the diversity of contemporary civilization, no matter how great the denial of God in the human world, so much the greater must be the Church's closeness to that mystery which, hidden for centuries in God, was then truly shared with man, in time, through Jesus Christ" (*Dives in Misericordia*, 15).

Benedict XVI: The Council and the post-Council: Love is at the heart of the Church's proclamation

"Following in the wake of the teachings of the Second Vatican Council and of my venerable Predecessors John XXIII, Paul VI, John Paul I, and John Paul II, I am convinced that humanity today stands in need of this essential message, incarnate in Jesus Christ: God is love. Everything must start from here and everything must lead to here, every pastoral action, every theological treatise" (*Homily, Basilica of San Pietro in Ciel d'Oro, Pavia*, April 22, 2007).

Francis: Mercy is the joyful force that leads us out of sin

"God is joyful! And what is the joy of God? The joy of God is forgiving; the joy of God is forgiving!... Here is the entire Gospel! Here! The whole Gospel, all of Christianity, is here!... Mercy is the true force that can save man and the world from the 'cancer' that is sin, moral evil, spiritual evil. Only love fills the void, the negative chasms that evil opens in hearts and in history. Only love can do this, and this is God's joy!...

"What is the danger? It is that we presume we are righteous and judge others. We also judge God, because we think that he should punish sinners, condemn them to death, instead of forgiving. So 'yes' then we risk staying outside the Father's house!" (*Angelus*, September 15, 2013).

"Jesus Christ is the face of the Father's mercy. These words might well sum up the mystery of the Christian faith.... Jesus of Nazareth, by his words, his actions, and his entire person reveals the mercy of God.

"We need constantly to contemplate the mystery of mercy. It is a wellspring of joy, serenity, and peace. Our salvation depends on it. Mercy: the word reveals the very mystery of the Most Holy Trinity. Mercy: the ultimate and supreme act by which God comes to meet us. Mercy: the fundamental law that dwells in the heart of every person who looks sincerely into the eyes of his brothers and sisters on the path of life. Mercy: the bridge that connects God and man, opening our hearts to the hope of being loved forever despite our sinfulness" (*Misericordiae Vultus*, 1-2).

Mercy Is the Heart of the Gospel

Over the past century, the popes have used different ways to express the essence of the Gospel message to the men and women of their time — for example, the Sacred Heart, the kingdom of God, mercy, etc. Here is a list of some of these ways in which they expressed it — a selection of passages where the popes themselves analyze these different yet parallel ways: they all lead to Christ, and have this as their common purpose.

Pius XI: His plan for establishing the kingdom of Christ

Pius XI pointed out that his plan for establishing the kingdom of Christ is closely related to the restoration of all things in Christ, as promoted by Pope Pius X, and by Pope Benedict XV's "work of peace."

"It is, therefore, a fact which cannot be questioned that the true peace of Christ can only exist in the Kingdom of Christ — 'the peace of Christ in the Kingdom of Christ.' It is no less unquestionable that, in doing all we can to bring about the re-establishment of Christ's kingdom, we will be working most effectively toward a lasting world peace.

"Pius X in taking as his motto 'To restore all things in Christ' was inspired from on High to lay the foundations of that 'work of peace' which became the program and principal task of Benedict XV. These two programs of our predecessors we desire to unite in one — the re-establishment of the Kingdom of Christ by peace in Christ — 'the peace of Christ in the Kingdom of Christ'" (*Ubi Arcano Dei Consilio*, 49, December 23, 1922).

Pius XII: *The proclamation of Christ is preaching devotion to his heart and his kingdom*

"In the very year which marks the fortieth anniversary of the consecration of mankind to our Redeemer's Most Sacred Heart, the inscrutable counsel of the Lord, for no merit of ours, has laid upon us the exalted dignity and grave care of the Supreme Pontificate; for that consecration was proclaimed by our immortal predecessor, Leo XIII, at the beginning of the Holy Year which closed the last century....

"It is only natural, then, that we should today feel profoundly grateful to Providence for having designed that the first year of our Pontificate should be associated with a memory so precious and so dear ... and that we should take the opportunity of paying homage to the King of kings and Lord of lords (1 Tm 6:15; Rv 19:6) as a kind of Introit prayer to our Pontificate, in the spirit of our renowned predecessor and in the faithful accomplishment of his designs, and that, in fine, we should make of it the alpha and omega of our aims, of our hopes, of our teaching, of our activity, of our patience and of our sufferings, by consecrating them all to the spread of the Kingdom of Christ" (*Summi Pontificatus*, 1-2, October 20, 1939).

Paul VI: Building a civilization of love means establishing the kingdom of God

"[We seek] a way that will be attractive to us and productive in cultivating and regulating a style and a plan for the renewal of our Christian life.... We were already fleetingly challenged when we set before us the plan to seek within the 'civilization of love' the moral, religious, and civic fruits of the Holy Year.... But there are other excellent and fruitful ways in which we can condense the genetic strength of a Christianity that is ever new and life-giving, like seeds that will develop one day in a splendid way.... In this important moment of our spiritual growth, we can aspire once again to the way that is at the origin of the Gospel message, the way that is always on our lips and in our hearts whenever we recite that great and familiar prayer, the Our Father, and make as our own the theme which Jesus himself first preached: 'Thy kingdom come' " (*General Audience*, January 14, 1976).

John Paul II: The kingdom of Christ is the kingdom of Divine Mercy

"How great is the power of Merciful Love, which, we await until Christ has put all his enemies under his feet, completely overcoming sin and destroying death as his last enemy! The kingdom of Christ is tension towards the definitive victory of Merciful Love, towards the eschatological fullness of good and grace, of salvation and life. This fullness has its visible beginning on earth in the cross and the resurrection. The Crucified and Risen Christ is the utter revelation of Merciful Love. He is King of our hearts.... This is, therefore, the kingdom of love toward man, of love in truth; and it is therefore the kingdom of Merciful Love. This kingdom is the gift 'prepared from the foundation of the world,' the gift of Love. It is also the fruit of Love, which in the course of the history of man and the world is constantly making headway through the barriers of indifference, selfishness, neglect, and hate; through the barriers of the lust of the flesh and the lust of the eyes and the pride of life (see 1 Jn 2:16); through the source of sin which every man bears within him, through the history of human sins and crimes such as, for example, the ones that weigh on our century and on our generation ... through all that!" (*Homily during Holy Mass at the Sanctuary of Merciful Love*, Collevalenza, 2, 6, November 22, 1981).

"Divine Mercy reaches human beings through the heart of Christ crucified: 'My daughter, say that I am love and mercy personified,' Jesus will ask Sister Faustina (*Diary*, p. 374). Christ pours out this mercy on humanity through the sending of the Spirit who, in the Trinity, is the Person-Love. And is not mercy love's 'second name' (see *Dives in Misericordia*, n. 7), understood in its deepest and most tender aspect, in its ability to take upon itself the burden of any need and, especially, in its immense capacity for forgiveness?" (*Homily, Mass for the Canonization of Blessed Maria Faustina Kowalska in St. Peter's Square*, April 30, 2000).

"The message of merciful love needs to resound forcefully anew. The world needs this love. The hour has come to bring Christ's message to everyone: to rulers and the oppressed, to those whose humanity and dignity seem lost in the *mysterium iniquitatis*. The hour has come when the message of Divine Mercy is able to fill hearts with hope and to become the spark of a new civilization: the civilization of love" (*Homily, Mass of Beatification of the Four Servants of God*, Kraków, 3, August 18, 2002).

Francis: To have a merciful heart like the Sacred Heart

"A merciful heart does not mean a weak heart. Anyone who wishes to be merciful must have a strong and steadfast heart, closed to the tempter but open to God. A heart that lets itself be pierced by the Spirit so as to bring love along the roads that lead to our brothers and sisters, and, ultimately, a poor heart, one that realizes its own poverty and gives itself freely for others.

"During this Lent, then, brothers and sisters, let us all ask the Lord: '*Fac cor nostrum secundum cor tuum*': Make our hearts like yours (Litany of the Sacred Heart of Jesus). In this way we will receive a heart which is firm and merciful, attentive and generous, a heart which is not closed, indifferent or prey to the globalization of indifference" (Message for Lent 2015, 3, October 4, 2015).

"The starting point of salvation is not the confession of the sovereignty of Christ, but rather the imitation of Jesus' works of mercy through which he brought about his kingdom. The one who accomplishes these works shows that he has welcomed Christ's sovereignty, because he has opened his heart to God's charity. In the twilight of life we will be judged on our love for, closeness to and tenderness towards our brothers and sisters" (*Homily, Canonization Mass, St. Peter's Square*, November 23, 2014).

Divine Mercy in the Life and Teachings of John Paul II

St. John Paul II stated that the message of Divine Mercy formed the image of his pontificate. Popes Benedict XVI and Francis have reiterated the centrality of mercy as found in the teachings of their predecessor.

Spreading devotion to Divine Mercy is a sign of the times

"It is truly marvelous how her devotion to the merciful Jesus is spreading in our contemporary world and gaining so many human hearts! This is doubtlessly a sign of the times — a sign of our 20th century. The balance of this century, which is now ending, in addition to the advances, which have often surpassed those of preceding eras, presents a deep restlessness and fear of the future. Where, if not in the Divine Mercy, can the world find refuge and the light of hope? Believers understand that perfectly" (*Homily, Beatification of Sister Faustina Kowalska*, 6, April 18, 1993).

The message of Divine Mercy forms the image of John Paul II's pontificate

"The message of Divine Mercy has always been near and dear to me. It is as if history had inscribed it in the tragic experience of the Second World War. In those difficult years, it was a particular support and an inexhaustible source of hope, not only for the people of Kraków but for the entire nation.

"This was also my personal experience, which I took with me to the See of Peter and which it in a sense forms the image of this pontificate" (*Address to the Sisters of Our Lady of Mercy*, Shrine of Divine Mercy in Lagiewniki, June 7, 1997).

The message of Divine Mercy entrusted to the third millennium to transform mankind

"What will the years ahead bring us? What will man's future on earth be like? We are not given to know. However, it is certain that in addition to new progress there will unfortunately be no lack of painful experiences. But the light of Divine Mercy, which the Lord in a way wished to return to the world through Sister Faustina's charism, will illumine the way for the men and women of the third millennium.

"Sister Faustina's canonization has a particular eloquence: by this act I intend today to pass this message on to the new millennium. I pass it on to all people, so that they will learn to know ever better the true face of God and the true face of their brethren.

"In fact, love of God and love of one's brothers and sisters are inseparable" *(Homily, Canonization of Blessed Faustina Kowalska, 3,5, April 30, 2000).*

Divine Mercy, the sole source of hope in the face of evil

"We wish to proclaim that apart from the mercy of God there is no other source of hope for mankind. We desire to repeat with faith, Jesus, I trust in you! This proclamation, this confession of trust in the all-powerful love of God, is especially needed in our own time, when mankind is experiencing bewilderment in the face of many manifestations of evil. The invocation of God's mercy needs to rise up from the depth of hearts filled with suffering, apprehension and uncertainty, and at the same time yearning for an infallible source of hope. That is why we have come here today, to this Shrine of Lagiewniki, in order to glimpse once more in Christ the face of the Father: "the Father of mercies and the God of all consolation" (2 Cor 1:3). With the eyes of our soul, we long to look into the eyes of the merciful Jesus, in order to find deep within his gaze the reflection of his inner life, as well as the light of grace which we have already received so often, and which God holds out to us anew each day and on the last day" (*Homily, Dedication of the Shrine of Divine Mercy at Kraków-Lagiewniki*, August 17, 2002).

Benedict XVI said that the words of Pope John Paul II's homily "summed up, as it were, his Magisterium, pointing out that the cult of Divine Mercy is not a secondary devotion but an integral dimension of Christian faith and prayer" (*Regina Coeli*, April 23, 2006).

John Paul II prays for the diffusion of the message of Divine Mercy

"Today, therefore, in this shine, I wish solemnly to entrust the world to Divine Mercy. I do so with the burning desire that the message of God's merciful love, proclaimed here through St. Faustina, may be made known to all the peoples of the earth and fill their hearts with hope.... May the binding promise of the Lord Jesus be fulfilled: from here there must go forth 'the spark which will prepare the world for his final coming' (see *Diary*, 1732). This spark needs to be lighted by the grace of God. This fire of mercy needs to be passed on to the world. In the mercy of God the world will find peace and mankind will find happiness!" (*Homily, Dedication of the Shrine of Divine Mercy at Kraków-Lagiewniki*, August 17, 2002).

The teachings of John Paul II on mercy, fruit of his pastoral experience in Poland, and his analysis of the twentieth century

"Likewise, the reflections offered in *Dives in Misericordia* were the fruit of my pastoral experience in Poland, especially in Kraków. That is where St. Faustina Kowalska is buried, she who was chosen by Christ to be a particularly enlightened interpreter of the truth of Divine Mercy.... I mention Sister Faustina because her revelations, focused on the mystery of Divine Mercy, occurred during the period preceding the Second World War. This was precisely the time when those ideologies of evil, Nazism and communism, were taking shape. Sister Faustina became the herald of the one message capable of offsetting the evil of these ideologies, the fact that God is Mercy — the truth of the merciful Christ. And for this reason, when I was called to the See of Peter, I felt impelled to pass on those experiences of a fellow Pole that deserve a place in the treasury of the universal Church" (*Memory and Identity*, 5-6, Rizzoli: New York, 2005).

St. Faustina's message, gospel of Divine Mercy written according to the perspective of the twentieth century

"To those who survived the Second World War, St. Faustina's *Diary* appears as a particular Gospel of Divine Mercy, written from a twentieth-century perspective. The people of that time understood her message. They understood it in the light of the dramatic buildup of evil during the Second World War and the cruelty of the totalitarian systems. It was as if Christ had wanted to reveal that the limit imposed upon evil, of which man is both perpetrator and victim, is ultimately Divine Mercy. Of course, there is also justice, but this alone does not have the last word in the divine economy of world history and human history. God can always draw good from evil, he wills that all should be saved and come to knowledge of the truth (see 1 Tm 2:4): God is Love (see 1 Jn 4:8). Christ, crucified and risen, just as he appeared to Sister Faustina, is the superior revelation of this truth" (*Memory and Identity*, 54-55).

Pope Benedict XVI on the message of mercy in the life of John Paul II: The power that imposes limits on evil in the world is mercy manifested on the cross

"[Pope John Paul II] has left us an interpretation of suffering that is not a theological or philosophical theory but a fruit that matured on his personal path of suffering which he walked, sustained by faith in the Crucified Lord. This interpretation, which he worked out in faith and which gave meaning to his suffering lived in communion with that of the Lord, spoke through his silent pain, transforming it into an important message....

"The Pope shows that he is deeply touched by the spectacle of the power of evil, which we dramatically experienced in the century that has just ended....

"Is there a limit against which the power of evil shatters? 'Yes, there is,' the Pope replies.... The power that imposes a limit on evil is Divine Mercy....

"In a retrospective review of the attack of 13 May 1981 and on the basis of the experience of his journey with God and with the world, John Paul II further deepened this answer. What limits the force of evil, the power, in brief, which overcomes it — this is how he says it — is God's suffering, the suffering of the Son of God on the Cross" (*Address to the Members of the Roman Curia*, December 22, 2005).

Pope Francis on the time of mercy: An intuition inspired by the Spirit and a gift of John Paul II

"[We are here] to hear the voice of the Spirit speaking to the whole Church of our time, which is the time of mercy. I am sure of this.... We are living in a time of mercy, and have been for 30 years or more, up to today. This was an intuition of Blessed John Paul II. He 'sensed' that this was the time of mercy....

"We cannot forget the great content, the great intuitions and gifts that have been left to the People of God. And Divine Mercy is one of these. It is a gift which he [John Paul II] gave to us, but which comes from above" (*Address to Parish Priests of the Diocese of Rome*, March 6, 2014).

CHAPTER TWO

The Sources of Divine Mercy

The preceding passages remind us that one thing is certain in recent papal teaching: the hearts of those living today — especially those of Christians — will turn to God if the Church is able to proclaim more clearly the merciful love of the Lord. For this reason above all, the pope encourages men and women of our time to seek the logic of mercy that is at work in the history of salvation, especially in the Paschal Mystery. In order to draw closer to God's love, we need to comprehend and experience the way in which God has intervened throughout history for the well-being of mankind, first and foremost on the cross.

Mercy Comes from God

Pius XII: Mercy and justice are joined together in the Paschal Mystery

"[The mystery of redemption] is a mystery of the love of the Most Holy Trinity and of the divine Redeemer towards all men. Because they were entirely unable to make adequate satisfaction for their sins, Christ, through the infinite treasure of his merits acquired for us by the shedding of his precious blood, was able to restore completely that pact of friendship between God and man which had been broken, first by the grievous fall of Adam in the earthly paradise, and then by the countless sins of the chosen people.

"Since our divine Redeemer as our lawful and perfect Mediator, out of his ardent love for us, restored complete harmony between the duties and obligations of the human race and the rights of God, he is therefore responsible for the existence of that wonderful reconciliation of divine justice and divine mercy which constitutes the sublime mystery of our salvation" (*Haurietis Aquas*, 36-37, May 15, 1956).

Paul VI: Human misery and Divine Mercy, the framework of salvation history

In the following text, Paul VI develops an insight from St. Augustine, which he referred to on several occasions and which he used in summarizing the history of salvation as the encounter of man's misery and God's mercy. This text provides an enlightening introduction to this section of this anthology. In Christ, the misery of sin and evil encounter God's plan of mercy, in which man participates through repentance.

"St. Augustine provides us with a formula, which is not only a formula in words, but a formula that is a human and theological reality encapsulated in two challenging words: misery and mercy. When we say misery, we are speaking about sin, the human tragedy that unfolds throughout the history of evil, that abyss of darkness that leads to horrendous ruin. Sin: ... the time has come to examine more clearly this concept, which plays an inferior and negative role in the whole Christian concept of human existence; it is all the more appropriate since the theoretical and practical ideologies of today's world are trying to expunge the name and the reality of sin from modern discourse. However, yet another truth emerges; another fate is reserved for man in order to attain the gratuitous, powerful, and mysterious plan of God's mercy. Divine mercy comes to rescue man from his misery. And you know how providential it is: 'Where sin increased, grace abounded even more' (Rom 5:20). And, you know how unpredictable this love was: Christ, the Word of God made man, took upon himself the mission of redemption. 'For our sake he made him to be sin who knew no sin, so that in him we might become the righteousness of God' (see 2 Cor 5:21). In other words, propitiation was offered in our place, earning for us restitution to a state of grace, that is, the supernatural participation in God's life.... In order to enter into this plan, we have to do penance, we have to know, accept, and live this economy of salvation once again. What could be greater, more necessary, and, ultimately, more beautiful, easier, and more fortuitous?" (*General Audience*, March 20, 1974).

"Focus your thinking, now more than ever, so that it will be habitually inspired by the mystery that is central to our entire faith, namely, the presence of the Son of God made man amongst us; the mystery of the Incarnation, which empowers us to truly repeat the name of Jesus, who was born of Mary and who dwelled in Nazareth, the name of 'God with us' (see Is 7:14; Mt 1:23). *Nobiscum Deus!* And then we will see ourselves rallying under this name, this name of Jesus, to the plan and to the reason for his coming into this world, the main reason why he appeared amongst us men and women, in the history of mankind: this is summarized in one name, a name that is so common yet so often profaned, that reaches to the highest heights of the deity; this name is love.... We must see the story of Jesus in this light: 'He loved me,' St. Paul writes, and each of us can and should repeat to ourselves: He loves me, 'and gave himself for me' (Gal 2:20)" (*Homily, Corpus Christi*, June 13, 1974).

"Redemption presupposes mankind's unhappy condition, the condition to which mankind is destined; it presupposes sin. Sin has an extremely long and complicated history: it presupposes Adam's fall; it presupposes the legacy of a state of privation of grace poured forth upon us at birth, the privation of any supernatural relationship with God; it presupposes a psychological and moral dysfunction within us that lures us into our personal sins; it presupposes the loss of that fullness of life to which God had destined us, which would surpass the needs of our natural being; it presupposes that there is a need for atonement and reparation, which are unattainable based on our own strength; it presupposes the warning of a relentless justice, a consideration in itself; it presupposes a still more pessimistic concept of the fate of mankind; it presupposes the defeat of life and the grisly triumph of death. It presupposes, or rather demands, a plan for divine mercy that is divinely restorative. At this point, then, the wonderful message of Christ coming into the world is proclaimed: *I have come!* (see Heb 10:5-10). Jesus came as the Savior, as the Redeemer, that is, as the one who pays, who makes amends for all mankind, for us. Let us try to fathom the meaning of this word: victim. Jesus comes into the world as a sin offering, the synthesis of the justice that has been fulfilled and the mercy that is reparative" (*General Audience*, March 29, 1972).

John Paul II: Christ makes the Father visible to us in his mercy

"In this way, in Christ and through Christ, God also becomes especially visible in his mercy; that is to say, there is emphasized that attribute of the divinity which the Old Testament, using various concepts and terms, already defined as 'mercy.' Christ confers on the whole of the Old Testament tradition about God's mercy a definitive meaning. Not only does he speak of it and explain it by the use of comparisons and parables, but above all he himself makes it incarnate and personifies it. He himself, in a certain sense, is mercy. To the person who sees it in him — and finds it in him — God becomes 'visible' in a particular way as the Father who is rich in mercy" (*Dives in Misericordia*, 2).

"The Cross on Calvary, through which Jesus Christ — a Man, the Son of the Virgin Mary, thought to be the son of Joseph of Nazareth — 'leaves' this world, is also a fresh manifestation of the eternal fatherhood of God, who in him draws near again to humanity, to each human being, giving him the thrice holy 'Spirit of truth.'

"This revelation of the Father and outpouring of the Holy Spirit, which stamp an indelible seal on the mystery of the Redemption, explain the meaning of the Cross and death of Christ. The God of creation is revealed as the God of redemption, as the God who is 'faithful to himself,' and faithful to his love for man and the world, which he revealed on the day of creation. His is a love that does not draw back before anything that justice requires in him. Therefore 'for our sake (God) made him (the Son) to be sin who knew no sin.' If he 'made to be sin' him who was without any sin whatever, it was to reveal the love that is always greater than the whole of creation, the love that is he himself, since 'God is love.' Above all, love is greater than sin, than weakness, than the 'futility of creation,' it is stronger than death; it is a love always ready to raise up and forgive, always ready to go to meet the prodigal son, always looking for 'the revealing of the sons of God,' who are called to the glory that is to be revealed. This revelation of love is also described as mercy; and in man's history this revelation of love and mercy has taken a form and a name: that of Jesus Christ" (*Redemptor Hominis*, 9, March 4, 1979).

"Indeed this Redemption is the ultimate and definitive revelation of the holiness of God, who is the absolute fullness of perfection: fullness of justice and of love, since justice is based on love, flows from it and tends towards it. In the passion and death of Christ — in the fact that the Father did not spare his own Son, but 'for our sake made him sin' — absolute justice is expressed, for Christ undergoes the passion and cross because of the sins of humanity. This constitutes even a 'superabundance' of justice, for the sins of man are 'compensated for' by the sacrifice of the Man-God. Nevertheless, this justice, which is properly justice 'to God's measure,' springs completely from love: from the love of the Father and of the Son, and completely bears fruit in love. Precisely for this reason the divine justice revealed in the cross of Christ is 'to God's measure,' because it springs from love and is accomplished in love, producing fruits of salvation. The divine dimension of redemption is put into effect not only by bringing justice to bear upon sin, but also by restoring to love that creative power in man, thanks to which he once more has access to the fullness of life and holiness that come from God. In this way, redemption involves the revelation of mercy in its fullness" (*Dives in Misericordia*, 7).

Benedict XVI: *The Cross reveals the gravity of sin and the transforming power of mercy*

"Contemplating the Crucified One with the eyes of faith, we can understand in depth what sin is, how tragic is its gravity, and at the same time, how immense is the Lord's power of forgiveness and mercy. During these days of Lent, let us not distance our hearts from this mystery of profound humanity and lofty spirituality. Looking at Christ, we feel at the same time looked at by him. He whom we have pierced with our faults never tires of pouring out upon the world an inexhaustible torrent of merciful love.

"May humankind understand that only from this font is it possible to draw the indispensable spiritual energy to build that peace and happiness which every human being continually seeks" (*Angelus*, February 25, 2007).

Francis: *Jesus is mercy incarnate*

"Jesus Christ is the love of God incarnate, Mercy incarnate" (*Regina Caeli*, April 7, 2013).

"After Jesus has come into the world it is impossible to act as if we do not know God, or as if he were something that is abstract, empty, a purely nominal reference. No, God has a real face, he has a name: God is mercy" (*Angelus*, August 18, 2013).

"With our eyes fixed on Jesus and his merciful gaze, we experience the love of the Most Holy Trinity. The mission Jesus received from the Father was that of revealing the mystery of divine love in its fullness. 'God is love' (1 Jn 4:8,16), John affirms for the first and only time in all of Holy Scripture. This love has now been made visible and tangible in Jesus' entire life. His person is nothing but love, a love given gratuitously. The relationships he forms with the people who approach him manifest something entirely unique and unrepeatable. The signs he works, especially in favor of sinners, the poor, the marginalized, the sick, and the suffering, are all meant to teach mercy. Everything in him speaks of mercy. Nothing in him is devoid of compassion" (*Misericordiae Vultus*, 8).

"When we look to the Cross where Jesus was nailed, we contemplate the sign of love, of the infinite love of God for each of us and the source of our salvation. The mercy of God, which embraces the whole world, springs from the Cross. Through the Cross of Christ, the Evil One is overcome, death is defeated, life is given to us, and hope is restored" (*Angelus*, September 14, 2014).

The Heart of Christ, Expression of God's Logic of Mercy

Devotion to the Sacred Heart is a pedagogical summary of how mercy comes from the Father, how it is perfectly revealed in the death of the Incarnate Word on the cross, and the way in which man can freely adhere to it. This devotion enjoyed immense favor in the preaching of the popes, beginning at the end of the nineteenth century and continuing until the 1950s. It is still relevant today since it is a synthesis of all Christian spirituality.

Pius XI: Contemplate the Sacred Heart to comprehend God's plan of mercy and in reparation for all sins

"Wherefore, even as consecration proclaims and confirms this union with Christ, so does expiation begin that same union by washing away faults, and perfect it by participating in the sufferings of Christ, and consummate it by offering victims for the brethren. And this indeed was the purpose of the merciful Jesus, when he showed his heart to us bearing about it the symbols of the passion and displaying the flames of love, that from the one we might know the infinite malice of sin, and in the other we might admire the infinite charity of our Redeemer, and so might have a more vehement hatred of sin, and make a more ardent return of love for his love.

"And truly the spirit of expiation or reparation has always had the first and foremost place in the worship given to the Most Sacred Heart of Jesus, and nothing is more in keeping with the origin, the character, the power, and the distinctive practices of this form of devotion" (*Miserentissimus Redemptor*, 11-12, May 8, 1928).

Pius XII: The Heart of Christ is a summary of redemption since it reveals God's mercy

"[In] the Heart of our Savior ... we can consider not only the symbol but, in a sense, the summary of the whole mystery of our redemption.

"Consequently, it is clear that the revelations made to St. Margaret Mary brought nothing new into Catholic doctrine. Their importance lay in this, that Christ our Lord, exposing his Sacred Heart, wished in a quite extraordinary way to invite the minds of men to a contemplation of, and a devotion to, the mystery of God's merciful love for the human race. In this special manifestation Christ pointed to his heart, with definite and repeated words, as the symbol by which men should be attracted to a knowledge and recognition of his love; and at the same time he established it as a sign or pledge of mercy and grace for the needs of the Church of our times" (*Haurietis Aquas*, 86,95).

Benedict XVI: Devotion to the Sacred Heart is an expression of the content of all true Christian spirituality

"Moreover, not only does this mystery of God's love for us constitute the content of the worship of and devotion to the Heart of Jesus, but in the same way it is likewise the content of all true spirituality and Christian devotion....

"Whoever inwardly accepts God is molded by him. The experience of God's love should be lived by men and women as a 'calling' to which they must respond. Fixing our gaze on the Lord, who 'took our infirmities and bore our diseases' (Mt 8:17), helps us to become more attentive to the suffering and need of others.

"Adoring contemplation of the side pierced by the spear makes us sensitive to God's salvific will. It enables us to entrust ourselves to his saving and merciful love, and at the same time strengthens us in the desire to take part in his work of salvation, becoming his instruments" (*Letter to the Superior General of the Society of Jesus*, May 15, 2006).

CHAPTER THREE

Mary, Mother of Mercy

God's merciful love is fully manifest on the cross, and it is from the cross that the power of the Resurrection is spread throughout the world, thanks to the Spirit. The entire history of mankind draws life from this source, Mary, the Mother of Mercy, the perfect example of new life created through divine love; the Church, which is the image of Mary; the Christian people, thanks to God's strength poured forth on the Church, especially through the sacraments; and the city of men, renewed through the work of the sons of God, who themselves have been transformed by mercy.

Paul VI: Mary was instituted by God to dispense his mercy

"Even if the grave sins of men provoke God's justice and merit his just punishments, we must not forget the he is 'the Father of mercies and the God of all comfort,' that he has appointed Mary most holy as the generous steward of his merciful gifts.

"May she who experienced the cares and hardships of earthly life, the weariness of daily toil, the hardships and trials of poverty, and the sorrows of Calvary, come to aid the needs of the Church and the human race" (*Mense Maio*, 11-12, April 29, 1965).

John Paul II: Mary experienced mercy and she works to spread it, at the foot of the cross and in the history of salvation

"Mary is ... the one who obtained mercy in a particular and exceptional way, as no other person has. At the same time, still in an exceptional way, she made possible with the sacrifice of her heart her own sharing in revealing God's mercy. This sacrifice is intimately linked with the cross of her Son, at the foot of which she was to stand on Calvary. Her sacrifice is a unique sharing in the revelation of mercy, that is, a sharing in the absolute fidelity of God to his own love, to the covenant that he willed from eternity and that he entered into in time with man, with the people, with humanity; it is a sharing in that revelation that was definitively fulfilled through the cross. No one has experienced, to the same degree as the Mother of the Crucified One, the mystery of the cross, the overwhelming encounter of divine transcendent justice with love: that 'kiss' given by mercy to justice" (*Dives in Misericordia*, 9).

Cardinal Joseph Ratzinger: Mary as the reflection of Divine Mercy in the message of mercy throughout John Paul II's lifetime

"Divine Mercy: the Holy Father found the purest reflection of God's mercy in the Mother of God. He, who at an early age had lost his own mother, loved his divine mother all the more. He heard the words of the crucified Lord as addressed personally to him: 'Behold your Mother.' And so he did as the beloved disciple did: he took her into his own home (see Jn 19:27) — *Totus tuus*. And from the mother he learned to conform himself to Christ" (*Homily at the Funeral Mass for Pope John Paul II*, April 8, 2005).

Francis: Mary is an expert in mercy, and her heart is in perfect harmony with Christ

"[Mary's] entire life was patterned after the presence of mercy made flesh. The Mother of the Crucified and Risen One has entered the sanctuary of divine mercy because she participated intimately in the mystery of his love.

"Chosen to be the Mother of the Son of God, Mary, from the outset, was prepared by the love of God to be the Ark of the Covenant between God and man. She treasured divine mercy in her heart in perfect harmony with her Son Jesus....

"At the foot of the Cross, Mary, together with John, the disciple of love, witnessed the words of forgiveness spoken by Jesus. This supreme expression of mercy towards those who crucified him show us the point to which the mercy of God can reach. Mary attests that the mercy of the Son of God knows no bounds and extends to everyone, without exception. Let us address her in the words of the *Salve Regina*, a prayer ever ancient and ever new, so that she may never tire of turning her merciful eyes upon us, and make us worthy to contemplate the face of mercy, her Son Jesus" (*Misericordiae Vultus*, 24).

CHAPTER FOUR

Mercy, Life of the Church

The divine river that flows forth from the Paschal Mystery reaches men and women through the channel of the Church, especially through the sacraments. After examining a quote from Pope Benedict XVI that gives an overview of mercy, other papal texts describe the Church as the place where mercy is poured out and where her shepherds play a unique role, particularly in administering the sacraments. Reconciliation merits special treatment since it speaks specifically about mercy. We will end this section, which is focused on the Church, with the holy years — a very exceptional time for rediscovering and spreading God's love.

An Overview of the River of Mercy in the Church

Benedict XVI: Mercy makes its entrance into history through Christ

"Indeed, mercy is the central nucleus of the Gospel message; it is the very name of God, the Face with which he revealed himself in the Old Covenant and fully in Jesus Christ, the incarnation of creative and redemptive Love. May this merciful love also shine on the face of the Church and show itself through the sacraments, in particular that of reconciliation, and in works of charity, both communitarian and individual. May all that the Church says and does manifest the mercy God feels for man, and therefore for us. When the Church has to recall an unrecognized truth or a betrayed good, she always does so impelled by merciful love, so that men and women may have life and have it abundantly (see Jn 10:10). From divine mercy, which brings peace to hearts, genuine peace flows into the world, peace between different peoples, cultures and religions" (*Regina Caeli*, Divine Mercy Sunday, March 30, 2008).

Francis: The great river of mercy

"From the heart of the Trinity, from the depths of the mystery of God, the great river of mercy wells up and overflows unceasingly. It is a spring that will never run dry, no matter how many people draw from it. Every time someone is in need, he or she can approach it, because the mercy of God never ends. The profundity of the mystery surrounding it is as inexhaustible as the richness which springs up from it" (*Misericordiae Vultus*, 25).

The Church as a Community Animated by Mercy

The Church, animated by divine mercy, does not jealously guard this treasure for herself, but offers it to men and women so that they may flee from the slavery of sin and follow the path leading to a new life. In this way, mercy is an essential key for all pastoral care.

Pius XII: The Mystical Body of the merciful Christ is also made up of sinners, who are called to repentance

"Nor must one imagine that the Body of the Church, just because it bears the name of Christ, is made up during the days of its earthly pilgrimage only of members conspicuous for their holiness, or that it consists only of those whom God has predestined to eternal happiness. It is owing to the Savior's infinite mercy that place is allowed in his Mystical Body here below for those whom, of old, he did not exclude from the banquet (see Mt 9:11; Mk 2:16; Lk 15:2). For not every sin, however grave it may be, is such as of its own nature to sever a man from the Body of the Church, as does schism or heresy or apostasy. Men may lose charity and divine grace through sin, thus becoming incapable of supernatural merit, and yet not be deprived of all life if they hold fast to faith and Christian hope, and if, illumined from above, they are spurred on by the interior promptings of the Holy Spirit to salutary fear and are moved to prayer and penance for their sins.

"Let everyone then abhor sin, which defiles the mystical members of our Redeemer; but if anyone unhappily falls and his obstinacy has not made him unworthy of communion with the faithful, let him be received with great love, and let eager charity see in him a weak member of Jesus Christ" (*Mystici Corporis Christi*, 23-24, June 29, 1943).

Paul VI: Mercy is the life that unites the Church and the world

"The fact that we are distinct from the world does not mean that we are entirely separated from it. Nor does it mean that we are indifferent to it, afraid of it, or contemptuous of it. When the Church distinguishes itself from humanity, it does so not in order to oppose it, but to come closer to it. A physician who realizes the danger of disease protects himself and others from it, but at the same time he strives to cure those who have contracted it. The Church does the same thing. It does not regard God's mercy as an exclusive privilege, nor does the greatness of the privilege it enjoys make it feel unconcerned for those who do not share it. On the contrary, it finds in its own salvation an argument for showing more concern and more love for those who live close at hand, or to whom it can go in its endeavor to make all alike share the blessing of salvation" (*Ecclesiam Suam*, 63, August 6, 1964).

John Paul II: Proclaiming mercy is one of the principal duties of the Church

"The Church must consider it one of her principal duties — at every stage of history and especially in our modern age — to proclaim and to introduce into life the mystery of mercy, supremely revealed in Jesus Christ" (*Dives in Misericordia*, 14).

John Paul II: The Church denounces sin because she knows that Divine Mercy offers its transforming power to man, who recognizes his own shortcomings

"If the Church, through the power of the Holy Spirit, can call evil by its name, it does so only in order to demonstrate that evil can be overcome if we open ourselves to *amor Dei usque ad contemptum sui* [love for God to the point of contempt of self]. This is the fruit of Divine Mercy. In Jesus Christ, God bends down over man to hold out a hand to him, to raise him up, and to help him continue his journey with renewed strength. Man cannot get back onto his feet unaided: he needs the help of the Holy Spirit" (*Memory and Identity*, 7).

Benedict XVI: Holy Church welcomes sinners who are called to repentance

"We believe that the Church is holy, but that there are sinners among her members. We need to reject the desire to identify only with those who are sinless. How could the Church have excluded sinners from her ranks? It is for their salvation that Jesus took flesh, died, and rose again. We must therefore learn to live Christian penance with sincerity" (*Meeting with Clergy in St. John's Cathedral in Warsaw*, May 25, 2006).

Francis: We can be transformed by God's mercy because we encounter Christ in the Church

"The Church enables us to encounter the mercy of God which transforms us, for in her Jesus Christ is present who has given her the true confession of faith, the fullness of the sacramental life, and the authenticity of the ordained ministry. In the Church each one of us finds what is needed to believe, to live as Christians, to become holy, and to journey to every place and through every age" (*General Audience*, 1, October 9, 2013).

Mercy does not aim to burden the faithful with certain customs that are not directly connected to the heart of the Gospel:

"St. Thomas Aquinas pointed out that the precepts which Christ and the apostles gave to the people of God 'are very few.' Citing St. Augustine, St. Thomas Aquinas noted that the precepts subsequently enjoined by the Church should be insisted upon with moderation 'so as not to burden the lives of the faithful' and make our religion a form of servitude, whereas 'God's mercy has willed that we should be free.' This warning, issued many centuries ago, is most timely today. It ought to be one of the criteria to be taken into account in considering a reform of the Church and her preaching which would enable it to reach everyone" (*Evangelii Gaudium*, 43, November 24, 2013).

"Being Church means being God's people, in accordance with the great plan of his fatherly love. This means that we are to be God's leaven in the midst of humanity. It means proclaiming and bringing God's salvation into our world, which often goes astray and needs to be encouraged, given hope and strengthened on the way. The Church must be a place of mercy freely given, where everyone can feel welcomed, loved, forgiven, and encouraged to live the good life of the Gospel" (*Evangelii Gaudium*, 114).

"There are two ways of thinking and of having faith: we can fear to lose the saved and we can want to save the lost. Even today it can happen that we stand at the crossroads of these two ways of thinking. The thinking of the doctors of the law, which would remove the danger by casting out the diseased person, and the thinking of God, who in his mercy embraces and accepts by reinstating him and turning evil into good, condemnation into salvation, and exclusion into proclamation.

"These two ways of thinking are present throughout the Church's history: *casting off* and *reinstating*....

"The Church's way … has always been the way of Jesus, the way of mercy and reinstatement. This does not mean underestimating the dangers of letting wolves into the fold, but welcoming the repentant prodigal son; healing the wounds of sin with courage and determination; rolling up our sleeves and not standing by and watching passively the suffering of the world" (*Homily, Mass with New Cardinals*, February 15, 2015).

"Mercy is the very foundation of the Church's life. All of her pastoral activity should be caught up in the tenderness she makes present to believers; nothing in her preaching and in her witness to the world can be lacking in mercy. The Church's very credibility is seen in how she shows merciful and compassionate love.… Perhaps we have long since forgotten how to show and live the way of mercy.… However, without a witness to mercy, life becomes fruitless and sterile, as if sequestered in a barren desert. The time has come for the Church to take up the joyful call to mercy once more" (*Misericordiae Vultus*, 10).

Mercy, the Foundation for the Life of Her Shepherds

As ambassadors of the Father of mercies and the servants of his brothers and sisters, priests are encouraged to embody charity and kindness in a concrete way. As holy clerics, the Church's ministers ought to share her greatest treasure: the mercy of the Father, a prophecy for a new world of brotherhood.

Francis: God's mercy renews the world

"St. Celestine V … like St. Francis of Assisi, had a really powerful sense of God's mercy, and of the fact that the mercy of God renews the world.…

"With their powerful compassion for the people, these saints felt the need to give the people the greatest thing, the greatest wealth: the Father's mercy, forgiveness. 'Forgive us our trespasses, as we forgive those who trespass against us.' In these words from the Our

Father, there is a plan for life, based on mercy. Mercy, kindness, forgiveness of debts, is not only a thing of devotion, of intimacy, of spiritual healing, a sort of oil that helps us be kinder, better, no. It is the prophecy of a new world: mercy is the prophecy of a new world, in which the goods of the earth and of work are equally distributed and no one lacks the necessary, because solidarity and sharing are the concrete result of fraternity. These two saints set the example. They knew that, as clergy — one was a deacon, the other a bishop, the Bishop of Rome — as clergy, both had to set the example of poverty, of mercy, and of totally divesting themselves" (*Meeting with Citizens and Proclamation of the Celestine Jubilee Year*, Isernia, July 5, 2014).

"Indeed, a pastor who is cognizant that his ministry springs only from the heart of God can never assume an authoritarian attitude, as if everyone were at his feet and the community were his property, his personal kingdom.

"The awareness that everything is a gift, everything is grace, also helps a pastor not to fall into the temptation of placing himself at the center of attention and trusting only in himself. They are the temptations of vanity, pride, sufficiency, arrogance. There would be problems if a bishop, a priest, or a deacon thought he knew everything, that he always had the right answer for everything and did not need anyone. On the contrary, awareness that he, as the first recipient of the mercy and compassion of God, should lead a minister of the Church to always be humble and sympathetic with respect to others" (*General Audience*, 2-3, November 12, 2014).

Mercy and the Sacrament of Reconciliation

The sacraments, especially the Sacrament of Reconciliation, are the means through which God's mercy transforms sinners and gives them new life. The popes have unceasingly encouraged shepherds to care for this ministry in a special way because "the priest is the sign and the instrument of God's merciful love for the sinner" (*Catechism*, 1465).

John XXIII: The example of the Curé of Ars

"St. John M. Vianney always had 'poor sinners,' as he called them, in his mind and before his eyes, with the constant hope of seeing them turn back to God and weep for the sins they had committed....

"From his experience in the tribunal of Penance, in which he loosed the bonds of sin, he understood just how much malice there is in sin and what terrible devastation it wreaks in the souls of men. He used to paint it in hideous colors: 'If we' — he asserted — 'had the faith to see a soul in mortal sin, we would die of fright.'

"But the sufferings of souls who have remained attached to their sins in hell did not add to the strength and vigor of his own sorrow and words as much as did the anguish he felt at the fact that divine love had been carelessly neglected or violated by some offense. This stubbornness in sin and ungrateful disregard for God's great goodness made rivers of tears flow from his eyes. 'My friend' — he said — 'I am weeping because you are not.'

"And yet, what great kindness he displayed in devoting himself to restoring hope to the souls of repentant sinners! He spared no effort to become a minister of divine mercy to them; and he described it as 'like an overflowing river that carries all souls along with it' and throbs with a love greater than that of a mother, 'for God is quicker to forgive than a mother to snatch her child from the fire.'

"Let the example of the Curé of Ars stir up those who are in charge of souls to be eager and well-prepared in devoting themselves to this very serious work, for it is here most of all that divine mercy finally triumphs over human malice and that men have their sins wiped away and are reconciled to God" (*Sacerdotii Nostri Primordia*, 90-94, August 1, 1959).

Paul VI: The Sacrament of Penance is not an automatic,
generous gift of God's mercy since it requires human cooperation

"This saving intervention of God's triumphant mercy requires some conditions on the part of the recipient, and we all know what they are. The effects of the Sacrament of Penance are not automatic or magical: it is a meeting where openness, receptivity, predisposition, as well as man's collaboration, are all assumptions.... We will now simplify the immense analysis to which this theme lends itself to mention the two key points of this aspect of Catholic penitential discipline. The first has a name that is difficult and painful, which is contrition.... It comes from an awareness, from which man usually tries to escape, an awareness of sin, which is based in faith in the relationship between our lives and God's inviolable and watchful law.... The other key point is confession, the indictment that man, eager for God's forgiveness, makes of himself, of his own faults, in full detail of their moral implications, to a minister who is authorized to listen to the penitent and administer absolution to him. What a tremendous thing, how tremendous penance is. So it seems to those who have experienced humility, who find truth and justice speaking within themselves, who have had the liberating, comforting experience of sacramental absolution. Perhaps the moments of a sincere confession are among the sweetest, the most comforting, and the most decisive moments in life" (*General Audience*, March 1, 1975).

John Paul II: Because of mortal sin, man rejects God's mercy

"It is to be hoped that very few persist to the end in this attitude of rebellion or even defiance of God. Moreover, God in his merciful love is greater than our hearts, as St. John further teaches us, and can overcome all our psychological and spiritual resistance. So that, as St. Thomas writes, 'considering the omnipotence and mercy of God, no one should despair of the salvation of anyone in this life.'

"But when we ponder the problem of a rebellious will meeting the infinitely just God ... in the light of ... passages of sacred Scripture, doctors and theologians, spiritual teachers and pastors have divided sins into mortal and venial....

"Mortal sin is sin whose object is grave matter and which is also committed with full knowledge and deliberate consent. It must be added ... that some sins are intrinsically grave and mortal by reason of their matter. That is, there exist acts which, per se and in themselves, independently of circumstances, are always seriously wrong by reason of their object. These acts, if carried out with sufficient awareness and freedom, are always gravely sinful" (*Reconciliatio et Paenitentia*, 17, December 2, 1984).

Benedict XVI: The formation of the confessor enables him to manifest renewing power of divine love

"With docile compliance to the Magisterium of the Church, he makes himself minister of the consoling mercy of God, he draws attention to the reality of sin, and at the same time he manifests the boundless renewing power of divine love, love that gives back life.

"Therefore, confession becomes a spiritual rebirth that transforms the penitent into a new creature. Only God's grace can work this miracle, and it is accomplished through the words and gestures of the priest.

"By experiencing the tenderness and pardon of the Lord, the penitent is more easily led to acknowledge the gravity of sin, is more resolved to avoid it in order to remain and grow in renewed friendship with him.

"In this mysterious process of interior renewal the confessor is not a passive spectator, but *persona dramatis*, that is, an active instrument of divine mercy. Therefore, it is necessary that to a good spiritual and pastoral sensibility he unites a serious theological, moral, and pedagogical preparation that enables him to understand the life of the person" (*Address to the Confessors of the Four Pontifical Basilicas of Rome*, February 19, 2007).

Francis: Without detracting from the ideals of the Gospel, we have to accompany with loving patience the journey of those who are opening themselves up to God

"Moreover, pastors and the lay faithful who accompany their brothers and sisters in faith or on a journey of openness to God must always remember what the *Catechism of the Catholic Church* teaches quite clearly: 'Imputability and responsibility for an action can be diminished or even nullified by ignorance, inadvertence, duress, fear, habit, inordinate attachments, and other psychological or social factors' (1735). Consequently, without detracting from the evangelical ideal, they need to accompany with mercy and patience the eventual stages of personal growth as these progressively occur. I want to remind priests that the confessional must not be a torture chamber but rather an encounter with the Lord's mercy which spurs us on to do our best" (*Evangelii Gaudium*, 44).

"It is normal that there be differences in the style of confessors, but these differences cannot regard the essential, that is, sound moral doctrine and mercy. Neither the laxist nor the rigorist bears witness to Jesus Christ, for neither the one nor the other takes care of the person he encounters. The rigorist washes his hands of them: in fact, he nails the person to the law, understood in a cold and rigid way; and the laxist also washes his hands of them: he is only apparently merciful, but in reality he does not take seriously the problems of that conscience, by minimizing the sin. True mercy *takes the person into one's care*, listens to him attentively, approaches the situation with respect and truth, and accompanies him on the journey of reconciliation. And this is demanding, yes, certainly. The truly merciful priest behaves like the Good Samaritan ... but why does he do it? Because his heart is capable of having compassion, it is the heart of Christ!

"We are well aware that *neither laxity nor rigorism foster holiness*" (*Address to Parish Priests of the Diocese of Rome*, March 6, 2014).

"A priest who does not foster this aspect of his ministry, both in terms of the amount of time he dedicates to it and in terms of its spiritual quality, is like a shepherd who does not take care of lost sheep; he is like a father who forgets his lost son and neglects to wait for him. But mercy is the heart of the Gospel!... Let us not forget that the faithful often find it difficult to approach this Sacrament, both for practical reasons and for the natural reticence in confessing their sins to another man. For this reason it is essential to prepare ourselves, our humanity, in order never to be an obstacle, but rather always to foster their drawing near to mercy and forgiveness" (*Address to Participants in a Course Sponsored by the Apostolic Penitentiary*, March 28, 2014).

"Among the sacraments, certainly reconciliation renders present with particular efficacy the merciful face of God: it is constantly and ceaselessly made real and manifest. Let us never forget, both as penitents and confessors: there is no sin that God cannot forgive. None! Only that which is withheld from divine mercy cannot be forgiven, just as one who withdraws from the sun can be neither illuminated nor warmed" (*Address to Participants in a Course Sponsored by the Apostolic Penitentiary*, March 12, 2015).

The Other Sacraments and Mercy

John Paul II: God's mercy spreads grace throughout the Church

"The Church has the mission of proclaiming this reconciliation and as it were of being its sacrament in the world. The Church is the sacrament, that is to say, the sign and means of reconciliation in different ways which differ in value but which all come together to obtain what the divine initiative of mercy desires to grant to humanity. She is a sacrament in the first place by her very existence as a reconciled community which witnesses to and represents in the world the work of Christ. She is also a sacrament through her service as the custodian and interpreter of sacred Scripture, which is the good news of reconciliation inasmuch as it tells each succeeding generation about God's loving plan and shows to each generation the paths to universal reconciliation in Christ. Finally she is a sacrament by reason of the seven sacraments that, each in its own way, 'make the Church.' For since they commemorate and renew Christ's paschal mystery, all the sacraments are a source of life for the Church and in the Church's hands they are means of conversion to God and of reconciliation among people" (*Reconciliatio et Paenitentia*, 11).

Benedict XVI: The Eucharist offers us the opportunity to experience Christ's divine strength in the gift of ourselves in serving others and in communion with them

"The Eucharist draws us into Jesus' act of self-oblation. More than just statically receiving the incarnate *Logos*, we enter into the very dynamic of his self-giving....

"Union with Christ is also union with all those to whom he gives himself. I cannot possess Christ just for myself; I can belong to him only in union with all those who have become, or who will become, his own. Communion draws me out of myself towards him, and thus also towards unity with all Christians. We become 'one body,' completely joined in a single existence. Love of God and love of neighbor are now truly united: God incarnate draws us all to himself.... A Eucharist which does not pass over into the concrete practice of love is intrinsically fragmented. Conversely ... the 'commandment' of love is only possible because it is more than a requirement. Love can be 'commanded' because it has first been given" (*Deus Caritas Est*, 13-14, December 25, 2005).

Francis: Baptism and confession, the intervention of divine mercy that forgives and that gives new life, and the Eucharist, bread of the needy who recognize their need of God's forgiveness

"In the Sacrament of Baptism all sins are remitted, original sin and all of our personal sins, as well as the suffering of sin. With baptism the door to an effectively new life is opened, one that is not burdened by the weight of a negative past, but rather already feels the beauty and the goodness of the kingdom of heaven. It is the powerful intervention of God's mercy in our lives, to save us. This saving intervention does not take away our human nature and its weakness — we are all weak and we are all sinners — and it does not take from us our responsibility to ask for forgiveness every time we err! I cannot be baptized many times, but I can go to confession and by doing so renew the grace of baptism. It is as though I were being baptized for a second time. The Lord Jesus is very, very good and never tires of forgiving us" (*General Audience*, 3, November 13, 2013).

"The one celebrating the Eucharist doesn't do so because he believes he is or wants to appear better than others, but precisely because he acknowledges that he is always in need of being accepted and reborn by the mercy of God, made flesh in Jesus Christ. If any one of us does not feel in need of the mercy of God, does not see himself as a sinner, it is better for him not to go to Mass! We go to Mass because we are sinners and we want to receive God's pardon, to participate in the redemption of Jesus, in his forgiveness" (*General Audience*, February 12, 2014).

The Jubilee as an Occasion to Rediscover and Spread Mercy

Paul VI: The Holy Year, an especially propitious time for concrete acts of charity

"My desire is that the Holy Year, with the works of charity it inspires in the faithful, be an auspicious time for solidifying a social consciousness within the faithful and within the wider circle of people that this message of the Church may reach.... It also seems that, in today's world, the problems that cause most concern and torment for mankind — economic, social, ecological, those concerning the energy sector, and especially those related to the liberation of the oppressed and the elevation of all mankind to a wider dignity of life — should be illuminated by the message of the Holy Year. But I want to invite all the children of the Church, and especially all the pilgrims who come to Rome, to make a commitment to several specific points that I, as the successor of Peter and head of the Church that 'presides over all in universal charity,' bring to the attention of all, namely, works of charity and faith in service to their brothers and sisters in need, here in Rome and in all the churches throughout the world" (*Apostolorum Limina*, 5, May 23, 1974)

John Paul II: The celebration of a Holy Year is a manifestation of divine mercy — for example, through indulgences and particularly through works of charity

"Another distinctive sign, and one familiar to the faithful, is the indulgence, which is one of the constitutive elements of the Jubilee. The indulgence discloses the fullness of the Father's mercy, who offers everyone his love, expressed primarily in the forgiveness of sins. Normally, God the Father grants his pardon through the Sacrament of Penance and Reconciliation. Free and conscious surrender to grave sin, in fact, separates the believer from the life of grace with God and therefore excludes the believer from the holiness to which he is called. Having received from Christ the power to forgive in his name (see Mt 16:19; Jn 20:23), the Church is in the world as the living presence of the love of God who leans down to every human weakness in order to gather it into the embrace of his mercy. It is precisely through the ministry of the Church that God diffuses his mercy in the world, by means of that precious gift which from very ancient times has been called 'indulgence.'...

"Reconciliation with God does not mean that there are no enduring consequences of sin from which we must be purified. It is precisely in this context that the indulgence becomes important, since it is an expression of the 'total gift of the mercy of God.' With the indulgence, the repentant sinner receives a remission of the temporal punishment due for the sins already forgiven as regards the fault....

"One sign of the mercy of God, which is especially necessary today, is the sign of *charity*, which opens our eyes to the needs of those who are poor and excluded. Such is the situation affecting vast sectors of society and casting its shadow of death upon whole peoples.... It is clear, therefore, that there can be no real progress without effective cooperation between the peoples of every language, race, nationality, and religion. The abuses of power that result in some dominating others must stop: such abuses are sinful and unjust. Whoever is concerned to accumulate treasure only on earth (see Mt 6:19) 'is not rich in the sight of God' (Lk 12:21)" (*Incarnationis Mysterium*, 9-12, November 29, 1998).

Francis: The Jubilee Year is an opportunity to attract all people to the path of love as the road to individual change and, therefore, social change. May the Church manifest throughout the Holy Year of Mercy her mission to give witness to mercy

"Here is the truly modern sense of the Jubilee Year, this Celestine Jubilee Year, which I proclaim open from this moment, and during which the door of divine mercy will stand wide open to everyone. It is not an escape, not an avoidance of realty and of one's problems, it is the answer that comes from the Gospel: love as a force of purification, of integrity, a force of renewal of social relationships, a force of planning for a different economy, which places the person, work, and family at the center rather than money and profit.

"We are all aware that this is not the way of the world; we are not dreamers, mistaken, nor do we want to create an out-of-this-world oasis. We believe rather that this is the good path for all; it is the path that truly brings us close to justice and peace. But we also know that we are sinners, that we are always tempted at first not to follow this path and to conform to the world's mentality, to the mentality of power, to the mentality of wealth. This is why we entrust ourselves to God's mercy, and we commit ourselves to carrying out with his grace the fruit of conversion and works of mercy. These two things: to convert oneself and perform works of mercy. This is the driving force of this year, this Celestine Jubilee Year" (*Meeting with Citizens and Proclamation of the Celestine Jubilee Year*, Isernia).

"I have often thought of how the Church may render more clear her mission to be a witness to mercy; and we have to make this journey. It is a journey that begins with spiritual conversion. Therefore, I have decided to announce an *Extraordinary Jubilee*, which has at its center the mercy of God. It will be a *Holy Year of Mercy*. We want to live in the light of the word of the Lord: 'Be merciful, even as your Father is merciful' (see Lk 6:36). And this especially applies to confessors! So much mercy!...

"I am confident that the whole Church, which is in such need of mercy for we are sinners, will be able to find in this Jubilee the joy of rediscovering and rendering fruitful God's mercy, with which we are all called to give comfort to every man and every woman of our time" (*Homily, Celebration of Penance*, March 13, 2015).

CHAPTER FIVE

The Christian and Mercy

Renewed by divine mercy, conformed to Christ through the Holy
Spirit, Christians are called to live up to the gift they have received,
by serving their brothers and sisters — especially through works of
mercy — and becoming an apostle of the Father's goodness.

Through the Father's mercy, Christians receive not only the
forgiveness of sin, but also, in Jesus Christ and through the Holy
Spirit, a new life: a life of kindness, conversion, forgiveness, justice,
of mercy given to others because it has been received from God.

The Merciful Lifestyle of Christians

Christians experience divine love when they encounter the Crucified Christ who offers them the gift of a new life transformed by
the power of the Spirit: they are able to better serve their brothers
and sisters and proclaim the Father's mercy.

*Pius XI: St. Francis de Sales is a model of this merciful way of
living*

"[St. Francis de Sales] was a model of sanctity. He was not a
gloomy, austere saint but was most amiable and friendly with all, so
much so that it can be said of him most truthfully, 'for companion-
ship with her [wisdom] has no bitterness, / and life with her has no

pain, but gladness and joys' (Wis 8:16). Endowed with every virtue, he excelled in meekness of heart, a virtue so peculiar to himself that it might be considered his most characteristic trait.

"Likewise, can we not hope that, through the practice of this virtue, which we rightly call the external sign of the inner possession of divine love, there will result perfect peace and concord both in family life and among nations?

"If human society were motivated by meekness, would this not become a powerful ally to the apostolate, as it is called, of the clergy and laity, which has for its end-purpose the bettering of the world?

"You can easily see, therefore, how important it is for the Christian people to turn to the example of holiness given by St. Francis, so that they may be edified thereby and may make his teachings the rule of their own lives" (*Rerum Omnium*, 6,28-30, January 26, 1923).

Paul VI: Sharing in the cross of Christ is to receive its fruit, which is mercy. By asking for forgiveness for our sins, we are responding to God's mercy

"Participating in the cross of Christ is to receive all the benefits the Cross has obtained for us, namely, God's mercy and, therefore, our salvation. This is the way in which the goodness of the Lord is revealed to us; he has chosen it in order to redeem us. He has opened his heart to us, and the love of God has been manifested to us, along with his desire to take our place vis-à-vis any responsibility for our failings and the punishments we should have had to endure for these failings. It is, therefore, the gift of mercy that we accept when we say that we want to take the cross of Christ into our arms" (*Homily, Via Crucis from the Coliseum to the Palatine Hill*, April 8, 1966).

"God's mercy is revealed to us: this economy of goodness should amaze us, astonish us, and even disturb us if we reflect on how much love has been poured out on us. Is it not, perhaps, his love that guides us in our lives?... We are able ... to believe that every sin and every attempt to flee from God lights up within him the flame of an even more intense love, a desire to win us back and reintegrate us in his plan of salvation. This revelation of mercy is something that is original in the Gospel. No one — whether through the human imagination or common phenomenology — could have thought of this" (*Homily*, June 23, 1968).

John Paul II: Man is in need of love and encounters it in the mercy that is revealed in Christ. Believing in mercy means believing that God's love, more powerful than sin, transforms man. One fruit of mercy in our life is conversion

"Man cannot live without love. He remains a being that is incomprehensible for himself, his life is senseless, if love is not revealed to him, if he does not encounter love, if he does not experience it and make it his own, if he does not participate intimately in it. This, as has already been said, is why Christ the Redeemer 'fully reveals man to himself' " (*Redemptor Hominis*, 10, March 4, 1979).

"Believing in the crucified Son means 'seeing the Father,' means believing that love is present in the world and that this love is more powerful than any kind of evil in which individuals, humanity, or the world are involved. Believing in this love means believing in mercy. For mercy is an indispensable dimension of love; it is as it were love's second name and, at the same time, the specific manner in which love is revealed and effected vis-à-vis the reality of the evil that is in the world, affecting and besieging man, insinuating itself even into his heart and capable of causing him to 'perish in Gehenna' " (*Dives in Misericordia*, 7).

"Conversion is the most concrete expression of the working of love and of the presence of mercy in the human world. The true and proper meaning of mercy does not consist only in looking, however penetratingly and compassionately, at moral, physical, or material evil: mercy is manifested in its true and proper aspect when it restores to value, promotes and draws good from all the forms of evil existing in the world and in man. Understood in this way, mercy constitutes the fundamental content of the messianic message of

Christ and the constitutive power of his mission" (*Dives in Misericordia*, 6).

"Mercy in itself, as a perfection of the infinite God, is also infinite. Also infinite therefore and inexhaustible is the Father's readiness to receive the prodigal children who return to his home. Infinite are the readiness and power of forgiveness that flow continually from the marvelous value of the sacrifice of the Son. No human sin can prevail over this power or even limit it. On the part of man, only a lack of goodwill can limit it, a lack of readiness to be converted and to repent, in other words persistence in obstinacy, opposing grace and truth, especially in the face of the witness of the cross and resurrection of Christ....

"Authentic knowledge of the God of mercy, the God of tender love, is a constant and inexhaustible source of conversion, not only as a momentary interior act but also as a permanent attitude, as a state of mind. Those who come to know God in this way, who 'see' him in this way, can live only in a state of being continually converted to him. They live, therefore, in ... this state of conversion" (*Dives in Misericordia*, 13).

"Christ — the very fulfillment of the messianic prophecy — by becoming the incarnation of the love that is manifested with particular force with regard to the suffering, the unfortunate, and sinners, makes present and thus more fully reveals the Father, who is God 'rich in mercy.' At the same time, by becoming for people a model of merciful love for others, Christ proclaims by his actions even more than by his words that call to mercy which is one of the essential elements of the Gospel ethos. In this instance it is not just a case of fulfilling a commandment or an obligation of an ethical nature; it is also a case of satisfying a condition of major importance for God to reveal himself in his mercy to man: 'The merciful ... shall obtain mercy' " (*Dives in Misericordia*, 3).

"Man attains to the merciful love of God, his mercy, to the extent that he himself is interiorly transformed in the spirit of that love towards his neighbor.

"This authentically evangelical process is not just a spiritual transformation realized once and for all: it is a whole lifestyle, an essential and continuous characteristic of the Christian vocation....

"In this sense Christ crucified is for us the loftiest model, inspiration, and encouragement. When we base ourselves on this disquieting model, we are able with all humility to show mercy to others, knowing that Christ accepts it as if it were shown to himself. On the basis of this model, we must also continually purify all our actions and all our intentions in which mercy is understood and practiced in a unilateral way, as a good done to others. An act of merciful love is only really such when we are deeply convinced at the moment that we perform it that we are at the same time receiving mercy from the people who are accepting it from us. If this bilateral and reciprocal quality is absent, our actions are not yet true acts of mercy, nor has there yet been fully completed in us that conversion to which Christ has shown us the way by his words and example, even to the cross, nor are we yet sharing fully in the magnificent source of merciful love that has been revealed to us by him" (*Dives in Misericordia*, 14).

Benedict XVI: Love for God is necessarily complemented by love for others. Divine mercy takes away our sins and also leads us on the path of new life

"If I have no contact whatsoever with God in my life, then I cannot see in the other anything more than the other, and I am incapable of seeing in him the image of God. But if in my life I fail completely to heed others, solely out of a desire to be 'devout' and to perform my 'religious duties,' then my relationship with God will also grow arid. It becomes merely 'proper,' but loveless. Only my readiness to encounter my neighbor and to show him love makes me sensitive to God as well. Only if I serve my neighbor can my eyes be opened to what God does for me and how much he loves me. The saints — consider the example of Blessed Teresa of Calcutta — constantly renewed their capacity for love of neighbor from their encounter with the Eucharistic Lord, and conversely this encounter acquired its real-ism and depth in their service to others. Love of God and love of neighbor are thus inseparable, they form a single commandment. But both live from the love of God who has loved us first" (*Deus Caritas Est*, 18).

"Divine mercy consists not only in the remission of our sins; it also consists in the fact that God, our Father, redirects us, sometimes not without pain, affliction, or fear on our part, to the path of truth and light, for he does not wish us to be lost (see Mt 18:14; Jn 3:16). This double expression of divine mercy shows how faithful God is to the covenant sealed with each Christian in his or her baptism" (*Address, Cathedral of Our Lady of Mercy in Cotonou, Benin*, November 18, 2011).

Francis: From the cross, the supreme act of mercy, we receive the power to be reborn as a new creation. The encounter with the merciful Jesus gives us the strength to start anew and to be capable of mercy

"Pastoral fruitfulness, the fruitfulness of the Gospel proclamation, is measured neither by success nor by failure according to the criteria of human evaluation, but by becoming conformed to the logic of the Cross of Jesus, which is the logic of stepping outside oneself and spending oneself, the logic of love. It is the Cross — always the Cross that is present with Christ, because at times we are offered the Cross without Christ: this has no purpose! — it is the Cross, and always the Cross with Christ, which guarantees the fruitfulness of our mission. And it is from the Cross, the supreme act of mercy and love, that we are reborn as a 'new creation' (Gal 6:15)" (*Homily, Mass with Seminarians, Novices and Those Discerning Their Vocation*, July 7, 2013).

"I invite all Christians, everywhere, at this very moment, to a renewed personal encounter with Jesus Christ, or at least an openness to letting him encounter them; I ask all of you to do this unfailingly each day. No one should think that this invitation is not meant for him or her, since 'no one is excluded from the joy brought by the Lord.' The Lord does not disappoint those who take this risk; whenever we take a step towards Jesus, we come to realize that he is already there, waiting for us with open arms…. No one can strip us of the dignity bestowed upon us by this boundless and unfailing love. With a tenderness that never disappoints, but is always capable of restoring our joy, he makes it possible for us to lift up our heads and to start anew. Let us not flee from the resurrection of Jesus, let us never give up, come what will. May nothing inspire more than his life, which impels us onwards!" (*Evangelii Gaudium*, 3).

"In short, we are called to show mercy because mercy has first been shown to us. Pardoning offenses becomes the clearest expression of merciful love, and for us Christians it is an imperative from which we cannot excuse ourselves. At times how hard it seems to forgive! And yet pardon is the instrument placed into our fragile hands to attain serenity of heart. To let go of anger, wrath, violence, and revenge are necessary conditions to living joyfully" (*Misericordiae Vultus*, 9).

"We want to live this Jubilee Year in light of the Lord's words: *Merciful like the Father*. The Evangelist reminds us of the teaching of Jesus who says, 'Be merciful just as your Father is merciful' (Lk 6:36). It is a program of life as demanding as it is rich with joy and peace. Jesus' command is directed to anyone willing to listen to his voice (see Lk 6:27). In order to be capable of mercy, therefore, we must first of all dispose ourselves to listen to the Word of God. This means rediscovering the value of silence in order to meditate on the Word that comes to us. In this way, it will be possible to contemplate God's mercy and adopt it as our lifestyle….

"If anyone wishes to avoid God's judgment, he should not make himself the judge of his brother or sister. Human beings, whenever they judge, look no farther than the surface, whereas the Father looks into the very depths of the soul. How much harm words do when they are motivated by feelings of jealousy and envy! To speak ill of others puts them in a bad light, undermines their reputation, and leaves them prey to the whims of gossip. To refrain from judgment and condemnation means, in a positive sense, to know how to accept the good in every person and to spare him any suffering that might be caused by our partial judgment, our presumption to know everything about him. But this is still not sufficient to express mercy. Jesus asks us also to *forgive* and to *give*. To be instruments of mercy because it was we who first received mercy from God" (*Misericordiae Vultus*, 13-14).

"God's mercy can make even the driest land become a garden, can restore life to dry bones (see Ez 37:1-14).

"So this is the invitation that I address to everyone: Let us accept the grace of Christ's Resurrection! Let us be renewed by God's mercy, let us be loved by Jesus, let us enable the power of his love to transform our lives too; and let us become agents of this mercy, channels through which God can water the earth, protect all creation, and make justice and peace flourish" (*Urbi et Orbi*, March 31, 2013).

The Works of Mercy

Pius XII: The essence of the Gospel is in works of mercy

"The very essence of the Gospel is in works of mercy (and the proof of this is in the very words of Christ the judge, who will admit into his eternal kingdom only those who have practiced mercy), and you, like all those who are directly called to relieve those who are afflicted in body and spirit, are called to be the living pages of this great book of God, called therefore to show the world that the message of Jesus Christ is not one without life, but the very substance of life, one that is always possible to be put into practice, one that can always be implemented, one that aims at converting the world from selfishness to love and one that gives — not merely as a promise — that comfort and that peace of which Jesus said: 'Come to me, all who labor and are heavy laden, and I will give you rest ... and you will find rest for your souls'" (*General Audience*, July 19, 1939).

John XXIII: Works of mercy are entrusted to women religious whose hearts have been widened through chastity. Works of mercy will change the world

"The Lord's holy Church is exalted ... and is embellished by the noble crown of her virgins, devoted to a life of prayer and sacrifice, and to carrying out the fourteen works of mercy.... On this occasion, we would like you to experience, especially as you face the world, the extremely high value and the splendor of virginity. It is the virtue which widens your heart to a love that is truer, vaster, and more universal, a love you can be given here on this earth: serving Christ in souls.... The special vocation of each religious family is rooted in this total consecration, which is expressed in serving God and serving your brothers and sisters, thereby unfolding an immense tapestry to beautify the house of the Lord, and on which are depicted — as we repeat so often — the fourteen works of mercy" (*To the Religious Women of Rome*, January 29, 1960).

[Facing the current crisis of civilization:] "We offer the works of mercy as the remedy to such deplorable abuses: we are certain that neither controversy nor debate, but only a Christ-centered and loving pride in publicly manifesting on a large scale the treasures of Christianity can stem the tide of evil. Look about you. On this sacred hill of the Vatican, the Church watches over immense treasures from centuries of art, history, and literature, but her most authentic treasures, and for which she has a maternal concern, are the poor, the sick, children, the weak, and the forgotten. It is for these that she raises her voice in supplication, appealing for understanding, protection, and benevolence. It is to these that she sends her legions of ardent and willing sons and daughters to wipe away tears, to console the spirits of the oppressed, and to support those who are suffering....

"The multiplicity of harmonious and productive endeavors that you represent today enables us to express the sweet hope that Rome, as a diocese and as the center of the Catholic world, may always merit the shining title that St. Ignatius attributed to it at its origins with incomparable praise: *præsidens universo cœtui caritatis*: presiding over all with charity, and be of this charity an example, an encouragement, and a beacon, as we have seen today, not giving precedence to one or a few, but to all the works of mercy" (*To the Delegates of the Works of Mercy of Rome*, 3, February 21, 1960).

Paul VI: *The pope is called to exercise works of mercy, both spiritual and material*

"What is the relationship between the two representatives of Christ: the poor and Peter?... Among the tasks of papal authority, the very first is that of exercising charity, which, as you know, is not only carried out through the so-called corporal works of mercy, but also, and above all, through spiritual works of mercy. And it is precisely these works of mercy that embody the specific content of the charitable and salutary mission of the apostolic office. This is also a reminder that if the pope is first of all a true follower of Christ, he must take the utmost care to help his brothers and sisters who are poor and suffering. He must be aware of the needs of others (see Ps 11:1), and, along with this awareness, compassion, and with this compassion, respect, and with this respect, the ingenuity to bring support to them in their need" (*General Audience*, November 11, 1964).

John Paul II: *Works of mercy are the most pressing tasks for the laity here on earth*

"Charity towards one's neighbor, through contemporary forms of the traditional spiritual and corporal works of mercy, represent the most immediate, ordinary, and habitual ways that lead to the Christian animation of the temporal order, the specific duty of the lay faithful.

"Through charity towards one's neighbor, the lay faithful exercise and manifest their participation in the kingship of Christ, that is, in the power of the Son of man who 'came not to be served but to serve' (Mk 10:45). They live and manifest such a kingship in a most simple yet exalted manner, possible for everyone at all times because charity is the highest gift offered by the Spirit for building up the Church (see 1 Cor 13:13) and for the good of humanity" (*Christifideles Laici*, 41, December 30, 1988).

Francis: Works of mercy point to the essence of the Gospel and awaken our conscience to the hardships of poverty

"I would like to highlight a particular aspect of this educational work of our Mother Church, which is how she *teaches us works of mercy*.

"A good educator focuses on the essential. She doesn't get lost in details, but passes on what really matters so the child or the student can find the meaning and the joy of life. It's the truth. In the Gospel the essential thing is mercy. God sent his Son, God made himself man in order to save us, that is, in order to grant us his mercy. Jesus says this clearly, summarizing his teaching for the disciples: 'Be merciful, even as your Father is merciful' (Lk 6:36). Can there be a Christian who isn't merciful? No. A Christian must necessarily be merciful, because this is the center of the Gospel. And faithful to this teaching, the Church can only repeat the same thing to her children: 'Be merciful,' as the Father is, and as Jesus was. Mercy" (*General Audience*, September 10, 2014).

"It is my burning desire that, during this Jubilee, the Christian people may reflect on the *corporal and spiritual works of mercy*. It will be a way to reawaken our conscience, too often grown dull in the face of poverty. And let us enter more deeply into the heart of the Gospel where the poor have a special experience of God's mercy.… Let us rediscover these *corporal works of mercy*: to feed the hungry, give drink to the thirsty, clothe the naked, welcome the stranger, heal the sick, visit the imprisoned, and bury the dead. And let us not forget the *spiritual works of mercy*: to counsel the doubtful, instruct the ignorant, admonish sinners, comfort the afflicted, forgive offenses, bear patiently those who do us ill, and pray for the living and the dead.

"We cannot escape the Lord's words to us, and they will serve as the criteria upon which we will be judged: whether we have fed the hungry and given drink to the thirsty, welcomed the stranger and clothed the naked, or spent time with the sick and those in prison (see Mt 25:31-45). Moreover, we will be asked if we have helped others to escape the doubt that causes them to fall into despair and which is often a source of loneliness; if we have helped to overcome the ignorance in which millions of people live, especially children deprived of the necessary means to free them from the bonds of poverty; if we have been close to the lonely and afflicted; if we have forgiven those who have offended us and have rejected all forms of anger and hate that lead to violence; if we have had the kind of patience God shows, who is so patient with us; and if we have commended our brothers and sisters to the Lord in prayer. In each of these 'little ones,' Christ himself is present. His flesh becomes visible in the flesh of the tortured, the crushed, the scourged, the malnourished, and the exiled ... to be acknowledged, touched, and cared for by us. Let us not forget the words of St. John of the Cross: 'As we prepare to leave this life, we will be judged on the basis of love' " *(Misericordiae Vultus, 15).*

Mercy and Mission

Paul VI: The mission to be bearers of divine mercy is binding on every Christian, even when they rediscover the values present in non-Christian religions

"Having discovered the values that are in non-Christian religions, human and spiritual values worthy of all respect, and having seen in these values a mysterious predisposition to the full light of revelation, is no excuse for a relaxed approach to the apostolate of the Church. On the contrary, it is comfort and encouragement. It is the recognition that God has other ways for saving the souls outside that pool of light, which is the revelation of salvation he projects on the world. This is no excuse for the children of light to leave it to God alone to carry out his secret economy of salvation, to forsake any effort on their part to spread this true light, and to excuse themselves from bearing witness, suffering martyrdom, and making sacrifices for their brothers and sisters, who, through no fault of their own, '*in umbra mortis sedent.*' Rather, God invites us to celebrate the mystery of mercy with a broader vision, with that of St. Paul: '*Conclusit enim Deus omnia in incredulitate, ut omnium misereatur*' (Rom 11:32), that is, to be the very bearers of this mercy on the widest human and historical scale possible" (*Address*, May 14, 1965).

Paul VI: God saves whomever and however he desires, but expects our participation in this mission

"It would certainly be an error to impose something on the consciences of our brethren. But to propose to their consciences the truth of the Gospel and salvation in Jesus Christ, with complete clarity and with a total respect for the free options which it presents — 'without coercion, or dishonorable or unworthy pressure' — far from being an attack on religious liberty is to fully respect that liberty, to which is offered the choice of a way that even non-believers consider noble and uplifting. Is it then a crime against others' freedom to proclaim with joy a Good News which one has come to know through the Lord's mercy? And why should only falsehood and error, debasement and pornography have the right to be put before people and often, unfortunately, imposed on them by the destructive propaganda of the mass media, by the tolerance of legislation, the timidity of the good, and the impudence of the wicked? The respectful presentation of Christ and his kingdom is more than the evangelizer's right; it is his duty. It is likewise the right of his fellow men to receive from him the proclamation of the Good News of salvation.... It would be useful if every Christian and every evangelizer were to pray about the following thought: men can also attain salvation in other ways, through God's mercy, even though we do not preach the Gospel to them; but as for us, though, can we gain salvation if, through negligence or fear or shame —

what St. Paul called 'blushing for the Gospel' (Rom 1:16) — or as a result of false ideas, we fail to preach it?" (*Evangelii Nuntiandi*, 80, December 8, 1975).

John Paul II: The apostolate of the Christian is to proclaim mercy as liberation from sin

"The missionary is invited to believe in the transforming power of the Gospel and to proclaim ... conversion to God's love and mercy, the experience of a complete liberation which goes to the root of all evil, namely, sin" (*Redemptoris Missio*, 23, December 7, 1990).

Francis: The language of mercy is expressed in gestures and attitudes

"We need Christians who make God's mercy and tenderness for every creature visible to the men of our day. We all know that the crisis of modern man is not superficial but profound. That is why the New Evangelization, while it calls us to have the courage to swim against the tide and to be converted from idols to the true God, cannot but use a language of mercy which is expressed in gestures and attitudes even before words" (*Address*, October 14, 2013).

"An evangelizing community knows that the Lord has taken the initiative, he has loved us first (see 1 Jn 4:19), and therefore we can move forward, boldly take the initiative, go out to others, seek those who have fallen away, stand at the crossroads, and welcome the outcast. Such a community has an endless desire to show mercy, the fruit of its own experience of the power of the Father's infinite mercy. Let us try a little harder to take the first step and to become involved!" (*Evangelii Gaudium*, 24).

"There is so much need of mercy today, and it is important that the lay faithful live it and bring it into different social environments. Go forth! We are living in the age of mercy, this is the age of mercy" (*Angelus*, January 11, 2015).

Mercy and the Christian Family

Family life is one of the most opportune places for Christians to experience mercy for one another in a concrete way. Christian couples rely on God's strength for this, especially through the Sacrament of Penance. To couples experiencing a crisis, the Church and its pastors are called to combine fidelity to God's plan for the family along with mercy for those who are suffering.

Paul VI: Mercy within family life: couples are called to have recourse to the Sacrament of Penance

"For this reason husbands and wives should take up the burden appointed to them, willingly, in the strength of faith and of that hope which 'does not disappoint us, because God's love has been poured into our hearts through the Holy Spirit who has been given to us.' Then let them implore the help of God with unremitting prayer and, most of all, let them draw grace and charity from that unfailing fount which is the Eucharist. If, however, sin still exercises its hold over them, they are not to lose heart. Rather must they, humble and persevering, have recourse to the mercy of God, abundantly bestowed in the Sacrament of Penance" (*Humanae Vitae*, 25, July 25, 1968).

"Now it is an outstanding manifestation of charity toward souls to omit nothing from the saving doctrine of Christ; but this must always be joined with tolerance and charity, as Christ himself showed in his conversations and dealings with men. For when he came, not to judge, but to save the world, was he not bitterly severe toward sin, but patient and abounding in mercy toward sinners?

"Husbands and wives, therefore, when deeply distressed by reason of the difficulties of their life, must find stamped in the heart and voice of their priest the likeness of the voice and the love of our Redeemer.

"So speak with full confidence, beloved sons, convinced that while the Holy Spirit of God is present to the magisterium proclaiming sound doctrine, he also illumines from within the hearts of the faithful and invites their assent. Teach married couples the necessary way of prayer and prepare them to approach more often with great faith the Sacraments of the Eucharist and of Penance. Let them never lose heart because of their weakness" *Humanae Vitae*, 29).

John Paul II: God's plan for the family and pastoral care full of mercy

"In the wealth of interventions, relations, and conclusions of this synod … there are two cardinal points — namely, fidelity to the plan of God for the family, and a pastoral way of acting which is full of merciful love and of the reverence that is owed to men, and embraces all of them, in what concerns their 'being' and 'living.' " (*Homily on the Theme of "The Mission of the Christian Family in Today's World,"* October 25, 1980).

"Together with the Synod, I earnestly call upon pastors and the whole community of the faithful to help the divorced, and with solicitous care to make sure that they do not consider themselves as separated from the Church, for as baptized persons they can, and indeed must, share in her life. They should be encouraged to listen to the word of God, to attend the Sacrifice of the Mass, to persevere in prayer, to contribute to works of charity and to community efforts in favor of justice, to bring up their children in the Christian faith, to cultivate the spirit and practice of penance and thus implore, day by day, God's grace. Let the Church pray for them, encourage them and show herself a merciful mother, and thus sustain them in faith and hope.…

"By acting in this way, the Church professes her own fidelity to Christ and to his truth. At the same time she shows motherly concern for these children of hers, especially those who, through no fault of their own, have been abandoned by their legitimate partner. With firm confidence she believes that those who have rejected the Lord's command and are still living in this state will be able to obtain from God the grace of conversion and salvation, provided that they have persevered in prayer, penance, and charity" (*Familiaris Consortio*, 84, November 22, 1981).

Benedict XVI: Justice, truth, and mercy do not stand in opposition to one another in irregular matrimonial situations
   "It is necessary to take note of the widespread and deeply-rooted, though not always evident, tendency to place justice and charity in opposition to one another, as if the two were mutually exclusive. In this regard, with reference more specifically to the life of the Church, some maintain that pastoral charity could justify every step towards declaring the nullity of the marriage bond in order to assist people who find themselves in irregular matrimonial situations. Truth itself, even if lip service be paid to it, tends thus to be viewed through a manipulative lens that would seek to adapt it, case by case, to the different requirements that emerge....

   "Today I wish to emphasize that both justice and charity postulate love for truth and essentially entail searching for truth. In particular, charity makes the reference to truth even more exacting. 'To defend the truth, to articulate it with humility and conviction, and to bear witness to it in life are therefore exacting and indispensable forms of charity. Charity, in fact, "rejoices in the truth" (1 Cor 13:6)' (*Caritas in Veritate*, 1). '*Only in truth does charity shine forth*, only in truth can charity be authentically lived.... Without truth, charity degenerates into sentimentality. Love becomes an empty shell, to be filled in an arbitrary way. In a culture without truth, this is the fatal risk facing love. It falls prey to contingent subjective emotions and opinions, the word "love" is abused and distorted, to the point where it comes to mean the opposite' (ibid., 3)" (*Address to the Roman Rota*, January 29, 2010).

Prayer and Mercy

   Prayer is one of those situations where Christians, in their dialogue with God their Father, discover in a concrete way the mercy of the Lord, both for them and for their brothers and sisters.

Paul VI: Prayer predisposes us to God's mercy

"Everything is dependent on God, because he is the first and only source of all things, even in the realm of human freedom; and everything is dependent upon man, insofar as he freely chooses his stance vis-à-vis God's action. In other words, God is the cause, man is the condition. Since God's action is carried out in a manner that is favorable to our interests, we must put ourselves in a situation — in a 'cycle' as today's language of mechanics would say — that would facilitate and enable God's merciful intervention. This effort to put ourselves into a situation that is favorable to God's work in us is called prayer. Prayer, therefore, is an integral part of our relationship with God and of the economy that is essential to our salvation. For this reason, the Lord highly recommended prayer to us, as if he were awaiting it from us in order to grant us his graces. It is the disposition that enables his mercy toward us" (*General Audience*, November 10, 1965).

"Gratitude is followed by repentance. The shout of glory to God the Creator and Father is followed by a cry for mercy and forgiveness. At the very least, this I know how to do: to invoke your goodness and confess through my guilt your infinite capacity to save. '*Kyrie eleison; Christe eleison; Kyrie eleison.*' Lord, have mercy; Christ, have mercy; Lord, have mercy. The story of my pitiable life comes to mind, interwoven, on the one hand, with a web of remarkable and countless benefits, arising from an ineffable goodness (and this is what I hope to see one day and 'to sing forever'); and, on the other hand, a mesh of poor choices that I would prefer not to remember insofar as they are so insufficient, imperfect, mistaken, foolish, and ridiculous. '*Tu scis insipientiam meam.*' God, you know my foolishness (Ps 69:5): my pitiable life — impoverished, stingy, narrow-minded, and so much in need of patience, reparation, and infinite mercy. It seems to me that St. Augustine sums it all: *miseria et misericordia*; my misery, God's mercy. At least now I can honor you for whom you are, the God of infinite goodness, by invoking, accepting, and celebrating your sweet mercy.... And then I ask myself once again: Why did you call me, why have you chosen me?

I am so inept, so reluctant, and so poor in mind and heart? I know why: '*quæ stulta sunt mundi elegit Deus ... ut not glorietur omnis caro in conspectu eius.*' God chose what is weak in the world so that no human being might boast in the presence of God (1 Cor 1:27-28). Being chosen points to two things: my own littleness; your merciful and powerful deliverance, which never ceases, even in face of my infidelities, my misery, and my ability to betray you" (*Thinking About Death [1965]* in *L'Osservatore Romano*, 32-33, August 9, 1979).

"And thus, with special reverence and recognition for the Lord Cardinals and for all the Roman Curia: Before you who surrounded me most closely, I profess solemnly our faith, I declare our hope, I celebrate our charity which does not die by accepting humbly from divine will the death which is my destiny, invoking the great mercy of the Lord, imploring the clement intercession of most holy Mary, of the angels and saints, and recommending my soul to the remembrance of the good....

"And concerning what counts most, my departure from this world's scene and my journey to meet the judgment and mercy of God: I would have so many, many things to say. On the state of the Church: May she listen to a few of our words, uttered with seriousness and love for her. Concerning the Council: May it be brought to a good climax and be executed faithfully. Concerning ecumenism: May the work of bringing together separated brothers proceed with much understanding, patience, and great love, but without defecting from true Catholic doctrine. Concerning the world: Do not think the Church can help it by assuming its thoughts, customs, tastes, but rather by studying it, loving it, serving it.

A complementary note to my testament [1972].... Some prayers that God may be merciful to me. In you, O Lord, have I placed my hope. Amen, alleluia. To all my blessing, in the name of the Lord. PAULUS PP VI Castelgandolfo, September 16, 1972, 7:30 A.M." (*Last Will and Testament* [1965-1972-1973], 1-6. The testament consists of the one written on June 30, 1965, with two complementary notes, one from 1972 and the other from 1973).

John Paul II: The Church implores through prayer for Divine Mercy to be poured forth on a world torn apart by sin

"The Church proclaims the truth of God's mercy revealed in the Crucified and Risen Christ, and she professes it in various ways. Furthermore, she seeks to practice mercy towards people through people, and she sees in this an indispensable condition for solicitude for a better and 'more human' world, today and tomorrow. However, at no time and in no historical period — especially at a moment as critical as our own — can the Church forget the prayer that is a cry for the mercy of God amid the many forms of evil that weigh upon humanity and threaten it. Precisely this is the fundamental right and duty of the Church in Christ Jesus, her right and duty towards God and towards humanity. The more the human conscience succumbs to secularization, loses its sense of the very meaning of the word 'mercy,' moves away from God, and distances itself from the mystery of mercy, the more the Church has the right and the duty to appeal to the God of mercy 'with loud cries.'...

"Let us implore God's mercy for the present generation. May the Church which, following the example of Mary, also seeks to be the spiritual mother of mankind, express in this prayer her maternal solicitude and at the same time her confident love, that love from which is born the most burning need for prayer" (*Dives in Misericordia*, 15).

The Political and Social Dimensions of Mercy

The popes envisioned the city of men as a place irrigated by mercy, especially through the conscientious efforts of Christians who have been formed by the Church and transformed by the sacraments. Let us briefly recall the principal points of what Pope Paul VI called the civilization of love.

Pius XII: The political dimension of mercy and prayer for peace

"Our God is love and charity itself, and we have experienced and believe in the love that God has for us (see 1 Jn 4:16). This is the mystery of the heart of God, the great mystery of Christianity.

God, in his infinite love and mercy, which is poured out upon all his creatures, will hear us — whenever and however he wishes in his blessed providence — if, at the foot of his throne, our trusting and ardent prayer rises up to him in one chorus, supported by our mortifications through penance, because it is part and parcel of the supreme eminence of goodness and divine love not only to pour out life and well-being upon all, but even more to munificently fulfill all the pious desires we express through prayer" (*Homily, Eucharistic Celebration for Peace in the World*, November 24, 1940).

Paul VI: The civilization of love is founded upon the Cross: Christ is loved and encountered in our brothers and sisters

"The wisdom of fraternal love, which is manifested in virtues and deeds that are rightly qualified as Christian, the historical journey of the holy Church, will explode with a new fruitfulness, victorious joy, and regenerating warmth. It will no longer be rooted in hatred, conflict, and greed, but rather in love, love that generates love, the love of man for man, not for any short-term, mistaken interests, not for any bitter and poorly tolerated condescension, but a love for you; a love for you, O Christ, revealed in the sufferings and needs of our fellow human beings. The civilization of love will prevail over the troubles caused by relentless social struggles, and lead to the transformation of the world of which we dream, a humanity that is finally Christian" (*Homily, Christmas Mass*, December 25, 1975).

"If we wish to inaugurate and promote the civilization of love, we should not delude ourselves that we can change these sad years on the banks of time into a river of perfect happiness…. Why do we refer to this distance of time and vision in achieving the true and perfect form of Christian life that has been entrusted to us? Oh, you know the reason, and it should not disturb our security or the joy we await and hope for. The reason is the Cross, erected at the highest pass between this present life and the future life. The Cross is not only a part of the mystery of love, but constitutes its very center, which we have chosen as the true and complete program of our renewed life" (*General Audience*, February 11, 1976).

"The synthesis between truth and charity touches upon some very important aspects of life, which can change it, as occurs often in the reality of history, into its antithesis! It is good that the recent council confirmed our commitment to both one and the other, namely, truth, which always merits our respect and, if necessary, the sacrifice of our lives to profess it, spread it, and defend it; together with the charity, the teacher of freedom, kindness, patience, and self-denial in our relationships with men and women, to whom the Gospel attributes the name of brothers and sisters. These are not plays on words, contrasts in schools of thinking, nor fatal tragedies of history; these are problems intrinsic to human and social nature, which are found in the Gospel, and therefore in the 'civilization of love,' whose humble and glorious solution we yearn for in the legacy of the Holy Year" (*General Audience*, February 18, 1976).

John Paul II: The civilization of love for which Paul VI yearned will become a reality if the message of mercy is embraced

"If Paul VI more than once indicated the 'civilization of love' as the goal towards which all efforts in the cultural and social fields as well as in the economic and political fields should tend, it must be added that this good will never be reached if, in our thinking and acting concerning the vast and complex spheres of human society, we stop at the criterion of 'an eye for an eye, a tooth for a tooth' and do not try to transform it in its essence by complementing it with another spirit. Certainly, the Second Vatican Council also leads us in this direction, when it speaks repeatedly of the need to make the world more human, and says that the realization of this task is precisely the mission of the Church in the modern world. Society can become ever more human only if we introduce into the many-sided setting of interpersonal and social relationships, not merely justice, but also that 'merciful love' which constitutes the messianic message of the Gospel" (*Dives in Misericordia*, 14).

*Benedict XVI: The civilization of love, which Paul VI
preached, has the purpose of making Christ's love visible while
courageously confronting ethical questions*

"His [Paul VI] was certainly a social teaching of great importance: he underlined the indispensable importance of the Gospel for building a society according to freedom and justice, in the ideal and historical perspective of a civilization animated by love. Paul VI clearly understood that the social question had become worldwide and he grasped the interconnection between the impetus towards the unification of humanity and the Christian ideal of a single family of peoples in solidarity and fraternity. In the notion of development, understood in human and Christian terms, he identified the heart of the Christian social message, and he proposed Christian charity as the principal force at the service of development. Motivated by the wish to make Christ's love fully visible to contemporary men and women, Paul VI addressed important ethical questions robustly, without yielding to the cultural weaknesses of his time" (*Caritas in Veritate*, 13, June 29, 2009).

Francis: Mercy is rendered concretely by serving the poor

"We incarnate the duty of hearing the cry of the poor when we are deeply moved by the suffering of others. Let us listen to what God's word teaches us about mercy, and allow that word to resound in the life of the Church....

"This message is so clear and direct, so simple and eloquent, that no ecclesial interpretation has the right to relativize it. The Church's reflection on these texts ought not to obscure or weaken their force, but urge us to accept their exhortations with courage and zeal. Why complicate something so simple? Conceptual tools exist to heighten contact with the realities they seek to explain, not to distance us from them. This is especially the case with those biblical exhortations that summon us so forcefully to brotherly love, to humble and generous service, to justice and mercy towards the poor. Jesus taught us this way of looking at others by his words and his actions. So why cloud something so clear?" (*Evangelii Gaudium*, 193-194).

"God is not only at the origin of love, but in Jesus Christ he calls us to imitate his own way of loving: 'as I have loved you, that you also love one another' (Jn 13:34). To the extent to which Christians live this love, they become credible disciples of Christ to the world. Love cannot bear being locked up in itself. By its nature, it is open, it spreads and bears fruit, it always kindles new love....

"Whoever experiences divine mercy, is impelled to be an architect of mercy among the least and the poor. In these 'littlest brothers,' Jesus awaits us (see Mt 25:40); let us receive mercy and let us give mercy!" (*Homily, Celebration of Penance*, March 28, 2014).